Teach®
Yourself

Successful Memory Techniques

Jonathan Hancock and Cheryl Buggy

www.inaweek.co.uk

Hodder Education

338 Euston Road, London NW1 3BH.

Hodder Education is an Hachette UK company

First published in UK 1999 by Hodder Education

First published in US 2012 by The McGraw-Hill Companies, Inc.

This edition published 2012.

Copyright © 1999, 2003, 2012 Jonathan Hancock and Cheryl Buggy

The moral rights of the authors have been asserted.

Previous editions of this book were published by Hodder in 1999 and 2003.

Database right Hodder Education (makers)

The *Teach Yourself* name is a registered trademark of Hachette UK.

British Library Cataloguing in Publication Data: a catalogue record for this title is available from the British Library.

Library of Congress Catalog Card Number: on file.

The publisher has used its best endeavours to ensure that any website addresses referred to in this book are correct and active at the time of going to press. However, the publisher and the author have no responsibility for the websites and can make no guarantee that a site will remain live or that the content will remain relevant, decent or appropriate.

The publisher has made every effort to mark as such all words which it believes to be trademarks. The publisher should also like to make it clear that the presence of a word in the book, whether marked or unmarked, in no way affects its legal status as a trademark.

Every reasonable effort has been made by the publisher to trace the copyright holders of material in this book. Any errors or omissions should be notified in writing to the publisher, who will endeavour to rectify the situation for any reprints and future editions.

Hachette UK's policy is to use papers that are natural, renewable and recyclable products and made from wood grown in sustainable forests. The logging and manufacturing processes are expected to conform to the environmental regulations of the country of origin.

www.hoddereducation.co.uk

Typeset by Cenveo Publisher Services.

Printed in Great Britain by CPI Group (UK) Ltd, Croydon, CR0 4YY

Successful Memory Techniques In A Week

Jonathan Hancock and Cheryl Buggy

The Teach Yourself series has been trusted around the world for over 60 years. This series of 'In A Week' business books is designed to help people at all levels and around the world to further their careers. Learn in a week, what the experts learn in a lifetime.

Jonathan Hancock gained two Guinness World Records for his remarkable memory and achieved the title of World Memory Champion. He used his learning skills to achieve a First from Oxford University, and has since published ten books on memory training.

Cheryl Buggy is a writer, lecturer and broadcaster. She runs a radio station in Portsmouth and writes programmes on emotional intelligence and releasing potential, for people of all ages.

Contents

Introduction

Memory is central to everything you do – and the great news is that it can be improved, quickly and easily. We've written this book to give you practical advice about taking control of every aspect of your memory and using it to the full, starting today.

When you know how to remember, how to tap into your brain's amazing power and apply it to all your learning needs, you feel confident about a range of challenges, at work and at home. You retain key information and access it easily, saving time and achieving more. Whether it's names, numbers, times, dates, individual facts or complex documents, you know how to remember everything you need, making you more organized and helping you in many different tasks. You impress people by remembering their names, improve your ability to communicate from memory, and do the right things to make other people remember you.

Memory training also helps your whole brain work better. The key techniques encourage you to organize your mind, improve your creativity and speed up your thought processes. You get a new awareness of what you can achieve, even under pressure, and see just how effective and enjoyable it can be to take charge of the complex set of processes that makes up your memory.

Small steps can make big differences. This book begins with a guide to adopting the right mindset, revealing how any negative thoughts that have been holding you back can quickly be replaced by a confident and open approach to memory. You may well have got out of the habit of engaging with information and enjoying the learning process, but that can easily change. By exploring how your memory works, and adapting your learning techniques to match, you can activate the full power of your brain and start making your mind do exactly what you want.

Most of the strategies explained in this book have been around for thousands of years, but they're more relevant than ever. All of them can make you better at the things you need to do today. You'll learn how to switch on your imagination, use the power of pictures, tell stories and go on mental journeys... to engage with the very real and important information you have to handle every day. Improving your memory is a fun process with seriously big benefits.

There are challenges we all face: dealing with the ever-rising tide of information, taking on new roles, coping with change. We also have our own particular learning needs, at work and at home, predictable and unexpected, enforced and chosen. Memory skills don't just help you survive the tests you face every day – they inspire you to set ambitious new targets, and to shine in everything you do.

In just one week you can start feeling different about your memory, and use it with a whole new level of confidence and skill.

SUNDAY

The right frame of mind

How you feel about your memory can have a big impact on how you use it. All your learning experiences up to this point have given you an opinion about your memory: the way you use it, how well it works, what sorts of things it can do. There will be some positive points, but it's likely that there are also plenty of negative ideas: for example, from the times when memory has felt hard or seemed boring or just plain let you down. It's easy to think that you've explored every avenue for your memory, when you've probably only scratched the surface; yet the thought habits are ingrained, and they're probably limiting the way you use your memory now.

If you can open your mind, you can re-evaluate your views and change your habits, breaking down barriers to learning that you may never even have noticed were there. It can seem like going backwards, because you may have to unlearn certain behaviours and recapture an approach that used to come naturally. But it's the way forward, and the necessary first step in setting up your thinking skills for success.

Brain power

There's never been a time when memory power was so important, and so neglected. It's undeniable that the workplace is changing at a pace never before witnessed. All of us are inundated with new information: new names, techniques, procedures, rules, facts, ideas. Stress levels are high, the need to communicate quickly and to think creatively is greater than ever – and yet few people feel mentally equipped to deal with it all.

How often do you hear or, worse, find yourself uttering the following mantras:

- 'I've got a terrible memory'
- 'I can't cope with this new software'
- 'I can't remember where I left that package'
- 'Everything's just too chaotic'

Stop. Within your head is more than enough brain power to cope with all the new data you face, all the changes you encounter in your working life. Your brain can deal with millions of pieces of information in the blink of an eye. You just have to use it properly.

Learn how your brain works, practise making it do what you want, and you can start tapping into its enormous potential.

The first step will always be to focus on the present – the way you try to think, learn and remember now. It's important to consider your current approach to learning, in order to highlight the bad habits and start focusing on the things that can be changed. Here's a learning task that you're unlikely to have to do in real life, but one that can help you to see the memory strategies you naturally employ.

> **How would you go about memorizing the following number?**
>
> **2821594434142463122635724**

You have one minute to learn as much of the 25-digit sequence as you can. When the minute has passed, cover up the numbers and see how much of the order you can recall. This chapter ends with a technique for remembering the whole sequence with ease; but let's begin by considering what might currently be stopping you making the most of your brain's potential.

Negative mindsets

You are the product of your experience. From childhood you've been on the receiving end of lessons, instructions, guidance and orders, from a number of sources. Parental influence led to that of teachers, your wider family, other adults, peer groups, and society at large. From that array of experiences, your view of yourself and the world has been formed.

The problem is, you almost certainly received far more negative messages than positive ones. Research suggests that, on average, 90 per cent of the messages a child hears are critical or negative. It's hardly surprising then that many adults have deeply rooted negative beliefs about themselves, and life in general. How often do you hear people say things like 'I'm not clever enough for that', 'I always failed in that in school', or 'I'm too long in the tooth to change' – and how often do you secretly agree with them?

> **'Whether you think you can or whether you think you can't, you're right.'**
> Henry Ford

One of the inevitable outcomes of a negative mindset is that you're setting yourself up for failure even before you start. In many cases, you never even try something: fear of failure keeps you trapped in a familiar – but limiting – 'comfort zone'.

Yet we've all read about or spoken to people who are not limited by negative thoughts, not held back by fear of failure, not frightened to try something new. Focus on your negative ideas and challenge them.

The latest research calls into question the assumption that memory automatically deteriorates with age. If you can use it properly and keep it in trim, your brain can do things you never thought possible – and *keep* doing them.

Habit

Humans are creatures of habit in what they do, and how they think. We like routine, doing things the way we've always done them – too often not the best way, just the way we've got used to. Generally we don't even realize that we're operating in an habitual way, cutting ourselves off from options that could dramatically improve our success.

Think of a habit you've broken in the past. A habit has to be learned, so it can be unlearned. It might have been tough, it might have taken a while, but remember the satisfying feeling of success when you achieved it.

To improve your mental performance, and to start learning and remembering effectively, you need to identify the ways of *thinking* that serve no useful purpose; thinking that might be holding you back; thinking that you would like to change.

As an example, imagine you'd decided to do something about your habitual failure to remember people's names. The process of change would be built on the following key steps:

- *Accepting that your thought processes are simply habitual*: you've got into the habit of forgetting, and have no extra memory strategies to help you out.
- *Telling yourself that this particular habit serves no useful purpose*: even when you struggle and strain to remember, you still fail to recall key names at the crucial time.
- *Acknowledging that you can change, because you want to*: a habit learned can be unlearned.
- *Knowing that you can change, however old you are*: ingrained habits are harder to shift, but it's never impossible. Remember, the longer you've failed at something, the greater the benefits will be when you start to succeed.
- *Seeing the advantages of change*: in this case you'd concentrate on the social and professional situations where remembering names is crucial. Imagine the feeling of confidence you'd enjoy, and the sort of impact you could have on others.
- Confirming to yourself that, from this moment on, you'll actively work on remembering names, using the techniques explained in this book.

Congratulations: you're on your way!

The way you've been taught in the past

When it comes to taking in new information, people have different natural tendencies. Three key learning 'modalities' have been identified:

1 **Visual** – seeing
2 **Auditory** – hearing
3 **Kinesthetic** – doing

SUNDAY

MONDAY

TUESDAY

WEDNESDAY

THURSDAY

FRIDAY

SATURDAY

Although we all rely on a mixture of the three, we have our particular, preferred learning styles.

Imagine you'd been given a barbecue kit to put together. How would you go about it? Would you read the instruction booklet? Would you ask someone to read the instructions to you? Or would you feel happiest simply playing around with the component pieces, exploring their construction through trial and error?

Your choice reveals a lot about your preferred modality. However, there are those who use all three to great effect. In doing so they're practising a form of holistic learning.

It makes sense to know which is your preferred modality so that, in any learning situation, you try hard to engage with information in that form.

It's also a good idea to practise other modalities in order to strengthen the learning and train your brain.

By taking a multi-modality approach, we can become progressive thinkers, creating a self-perpetuating circle of creative, challenging thoughts and positive feelings about ourselves.

To recap:

You have at your disposal an enormously exciting mechanism for learning and remembering – your amazing brain. But you may well be limiting your brain power because of:

- a negative mindset
- force of habit
- trying to use it in the wrong way.

So much for blockages to remembering and learning. What are the steps forward – the starting points for making this book work for you?

You need to be motivated

You won't succeed in anything if you can't see what's in it for you. Just as an athlete limbers up before an event and focuses on the goal, before you begin your journey to effective memory you need to prepare yourself mentally.

What will you get out of improving your brain? Your list might include:

- dealing with information more quickly and more effectively
- saving time
- impressing others
- enjoying learning
- using new skills to boost promotion prospects
- increasing confidence.

Spend a few minutes compiling your own motivating list, and make a point of looking back at it regularly.

You need a multi-faceted approach to learning

There was a time when we knew instinctively how to get it right. Think about the ways small children assimilate new information. They:

- engage all their senses
- give their imagination free rein
- ask lots of questions
- have little or no concept of failure

- remain enthusiastic and positive
- become totally engrossed in an activity
- try a variety of approaches.

This is sometimes called 'global learning', since it involves the whole brain: the left, logical side, which deals with organized thinking, decisions and lists; and the right, random side, which attends to imagination, creativity, pictures and ideas.

As adults, we tend to limit our thinking processes, designating one thing as a problem requiring logic, and another as a challenge requiring imagination. The trick to effective memory and learning is to use both sides at once, and to benefit from all the options available.

You need the right learning environment

Today's workplace is often open-plan, busy, full of noise, movement and interruptions. It's fine if you can concentrate in that sort of environment – some people even prefer it – but it makes it difficult for those who need peace and quiet to think effectively. Just as we all take in information in different ways, we also have our own preferred places and conditions for learning.

Whenever possible, you need to take control of your learning environment. What sort of place would be ideal for you? Would it be:

- noisy or quiet?
- a small room or a large, open office?
- inside or out?
- heated or air-conditioned?

Experiment with the conditions, and be aware of all the tricks at your disposal for boosting focus and concentration.

- Tackle important information when you're most alert.
- Let people know when you need private time and space to think.
- See if a particular kind of music boosts your thinking power.

SUNDAY

MONDAY

TUESDAY

WEDNESDAY

THURSDAY

FRIDAY

SATURDAY

- Surround yourself with visual images that please you, and be aware of how colours affect your mood.
- Keep your workplace as organized and as calm as possible.

You need to practise

All too often we abandon something without giving it a fair chance of working. We don't try as hard as we might to change an old habit and replace it with a new strategy, and reach for excuses to avoid practising it and putting in the work: 'I'm too busy', 'It's too difficult', 'Nothing's happening'. Suddenly the old, safe ways seem very appealing.

There's no magic wand or instant fix. Look back at your 'motivations' list – the things you could get out of having a powerful brain. Isn't it worth a little effort?

PMA – Positive Mental Attitude

We've already highlighted the debilitating effect of the negative drip-feed many of us have been on. The following points will help you start to change negative into positive, and begin building the right attitude to learning.

Remember:

- change is possible
- the techniques for tapping into your true mental potential are simple to learn
- learning can be fun
- the benefits of a trained brain are immense.

Stop:

- limiting yourself
- talking yourself down
- expecting failure.

Start:

- trusting in your abilities
- seeing problems as challenges
- enjoying the rewards of your efforts.

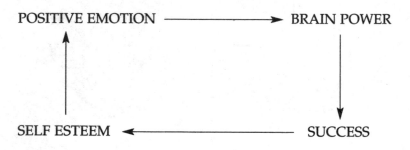

So, you need to ask yourself five key questions:

1 What's in this for me?
2 How do I learn best?
3 Where do I find learning easiest?

4 How can I start to practise?

5 How can I boost my beneficial thoughts?

Answer each of these questions in a positive way and you take a big step towards becoming a powerful and effective learner.

Learning habits may be deeply ingrained, but they can be changed – and when they are, the results are dramatic.

Near the start of this chapter you tried to learn a sequence of digits, using the approach that came naturally to you. Now, try learning it in a different way. It's possible to change information: to make it memorable. In this case, changing the numbers into words. All you need is to remember the first two lines of a couple of very famous songs:

'I'm dreaming of a white Christmas,

Just like the ones I used to know'

and

'Should old acquaintance be forgot

And never brought to mind'.

Spend a few moments repeating the lyrics from memory, checking you can recall them accurately. If you can, then you now know the complete number sequence. Simply write down the number of letters in each word.

'I'm' has two letters, so you write down 2.

'Dreaming' has eight letters, so the next number in the sequence is 8. 'Of' has two letters, so next you write down 2... and so on. See how quickly you can write out the entire 25-digit number from memory.

This is clearly an artificial experiment, but it proves an important point. By adopting the right frame of mind, and showing a willingness to learn in a new way and to change information into a more memorable form, you can remember anything. It's even easier when you're motivated, and learning real information that's useful to you.

You've made a commitment to finding new and improved learning techniques – and now it's time to get to grips with how your memory works.

Summary

To round off today, plan your targets for the future – they need to be realistic but also aspirational, reflecting your growing confidence in what you might be able to achieve.

Think about how you'd like to feel about your memory. What would it be like to have confidence in your memory skills generally, but also to succeed at particular tasks? Choose one area of your life where memory is a problem and imagine yourself in control, enjoying the benefits of a trained brain.

Next, consider some of the rewards of memory improvement. Which aspects of your life would benefit most from stronger learning skills? How exactly would the pay-offs appear? Think about things like time saved, stress reduced, promotion, better pay – and impressive results.

Finally, just how good do you want your memory to be? Which are the main areas you want to work on, and how will you benchmark your improvement? You might want to be able to memorize a phone number without writing it down, recall five work tasks, or give a ten-minute talk from memory. Your targets can change in time, but setting some clear goals now will focus your efforts and boost your motivation to give memory your best shot.

SUNDAY

MONDAY

TUESDAY

WEDNESDAY

THURSDAY

FRIDAY

SATURDAY

Quick-check

SUNDAY
MONDAY
TUESDAY
WEDNESDAY
THURSDAY
FRIDAY
SATURDAY

The following questions are designed to help you set your priorities for the rest of the week:

1. Which of the following areas of memory do you worry about most?
    a) Memory loss with age ❑
    b) Forgetting facts and figures ❑
    c) Losing possessions ❑
    d) Failing exams ❑

2. When you were at school, how good was your memory?
    a) Can't remember ❑
    b) Poor ❑
    c) OK ❑
    d) Strong ❑

3. How confident are you about learning new skills?
    a) Not at all ❑
    b) Unsure ❑
    c) Fairly ❑
    d) Very ❑

4. How good are you at remembering names and faces?
    a) Terrible ❑
    b) Not bad ❑
    c) Confident ❑
    d) Perfect ❑

5. What state is your mind in at the moment?
    a) Chaotic ❑
    b) Untidy ❑
    c) Quite neat ❑
    d) Well-organized ❑

6. How do you feel about inventing creative stories?
    a) Negative ❑
    b) Uncertain ❑
    c) Interested ❑
    d) Excited ❑

7. Which of these skills would you like to improve most?
    a) Speaking from memory ❑
    b) Revising for tests ❑
    c) Remembering people ❑
    d) Learning facts ❑

8. How often does your faulty memory cause you big problems?
    a) Regularly ❑
    b) Often ❑
    c) Occasionally ❑
    d) Never ❑

9. How memorable do you think you are to others, as a writer and speaker?
    a) Not at all ❑
    b) Slightly ❑
    c) Reasonably ❑
    d) Very ❑

10. How much confidence do you have in your ability to train your memory?
    a) None ❑
    b) A little ❑
    c) Quite a lot ❑
    d) A great deal ❑

MONDAY

Your amazing brain

Whatever you've come to feel about your memory, advertising agencies know that you have an amazing capacity to learn and remember – as long as the right things happen to activate it. At the start of Monday, spend a moment thinking about a few adverts that have stuck in your mind: on TV, at the cinema, in magazines or on billboards. Whether or not you've actually bought these products or heeded the messages, these communications have worked because they've created lasting memories. So how did they do that?

- They must have captured your attention in some way. How?
- They probably engaged with several of your senses. Which ones?
- They're likely to have triggered your short-term memory. With what?
- Their creators have worked hard to make your memory work. What did they do?

As well as remembering these adverts, see where your memories go next. When you first saw them, how did you feel, where were you living, what was your life like? Use the adverts as starting points and see what other information comes to mind. Start exploring your unpredictable, interconnected memory, ready to begin the process of learning how it works – and adopting the habits that will make it do what you want.

Your approach to learning

What's *your* approach to learning? Like Lincoln sharpening his axe, how do you prepare for a memory task, to make it as easy, enjoyable and efficient as possible?

Imagine you had to learn the following shopping list of ten simple items:

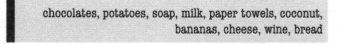

chocolates, potatoes, soap, milk, paper towels, coconut,
bananas, cheese, wine, bread

Spend a few moments now trying to learn this list as you would normally. As you do so, make an effort to notice what you're doing. What habits have you picked up? How do you try to remember?

By the end of today, you'll be able to learn a list like this with ease, and recall the items forwards or backwards. In fact, you'll be capable of learning a list twice as long.

To learn how to do that, you need to understand how your memory works. We'll examine the physical mechanisms of the human brain, to get a glimpse of how this amazing resource works, and how it must be fuelled and operated.

First, though, we need to ask a fundamental question: Why does it work sometimes, but not always?

Factors affecting recall

Almost everyone claims to have a terrible memory, but they don't seem to think that it's *always* terrible. In fact, they're in no doubt that it works very well for them sometimes.

A man who forgets his wife's birthday every year may be a doctor with a mental database crammed with thousands of medical facts. A woman who says that she can't remember telephone numbers could easily be a keen musician, and know countless pieces of music off by heart.

One of the most important steps in memory improvement is simply realizing that some things are easier to remember than others. Our brains do work, and we demonstrate our learning skills many times every day – but not every type of information sticks easily. Like Lincoln and his axe, you need to invest time preparing for the task, altering information to make it memorable.

We do this already. Everyone at some time will have made use of mnemonic tricks. 'Thirty days hath September'; 'Every Good Boy Deserves Favour '; 'Richard Of York Gave Battle In Vain'. Perhaps you remember certain numbers by spotting patterns, noticing significant digits – your age, for example, or your house number. Unfortunately, few people ever get to know about the really powerful memory techniques – the ones that let you change *any* kind of information to make it compatible with the way your mind works.

To discover what they are, you need to test your memory. Use the following experiment to find out the characteristics a piece of information needs to have if it's going to be memorable. Read through this list of 25 words once or, if possible, get someone to read them out to you. As soon as the list is finished, see how many of the words you can write down from memory, in any order.

> shoe, watch, flower, Madonna, chair, lion, kettle, ball, pin, firework, pencil, tiger, phone, warm, puma, hill, time, sharpener, mugger, cheetah, hat, car, apple, book, kite

What's most interesting about this test isn't how many words you remember – but which ones. It's possible to predict with surprising accuracy which words most people recall.

book, kite – you're likely to have remembered the last two words on the list because there was very little time to forget them. No new words appeared to confuse you, so you were able to carry them in your short-term memory for long enough to write them down.

shoe, watch, flower – the words from the very start of the list are also likely to have stayed with you. When the experiment began, your mind was fresh and alert. You were interested in the sorts of word that might be included, and it's likely that you were making a special effort to remember.

On the other hand, the words from the middle of the list are a great deal harder to recall. Your interest wanes, your mental energy drops, your concentration wavers and the whole task just seems too difficult and confusing.

lion, tiger, puma, cheetah – most people who try this test spot the four linked words – the big cats – and remember them all as a group. Perhaps you found that this also worked for *pencil* and *sharpener* – two words that you could easily link together in your mind.

Madonna – when a words stands out from a set of information, is noticeable and unusual, it's much easier to remember.

firework – being able to picture a word is a vital part of remembering it. In this case, the word also conjures up sounds and even smells, making it particularly powerful, especially compared with the abstract words in the list such as *warm* and *time*.

mugger – this word is likely to have provoked an emotional response, making it much more memorable than bland words such as *pin*, *phone* and *hill*.

From this simple test, key factors about memory are revealed.

You remember:

● when your mind is alert, you're interested and motivated, especially at the start and end of any learning period
● when material is patterned or connected
● when information is unusual
● when you can picture what you have to learn
● when the information makes you feel something.

You forget:

● when you lose interest and motivation, especially in the middle of a learning period
● when the material has no shape or connections
● when information is dull
● when it's difficult to picture the material
● when what you're learning doesn't provoke any emotional response.

If you consider these points in terms of your day-to-day memory experiences, you'll see that they make sense. The sort of information you tend to remember is:

● material you're interested in, or really motivated to learn, such as statistics about your favourite sport, or material to help you make money
● songs, tunes and poems – connected into memorable patterns of sound and rhythm

- stories, also based on connections, with one event causing another, one scene linking to the next
- faces – you know you've seen a person before
- unusual events – the days when you did something out of the ordinary
- embarrassing moments, times of happiness, fear, surprise – all occasions made memorable by strong emotions.

Of course, most information we have to learn doesn't conform to these points. We waste so much time struggling to remember things that – as they're presented – simply aren't memorable:

- numbers – abstract, hard to visualize or connect
- names – you recognize the face, but what's the name? Again, the name is abstract, easily confused and forgotten.
- everyday jobs – you don't feel particularly motivated, the information is dull and uninspiring, and so you regularly forget it.

So the best-kept secret of memory is this: if information is difficult to learn, you need to change it, to make it memorable.

Making it memorable

It may well be a step that you've never really considered before, but it will revolutionize your learning. Learn something well enough the first time, and that's it – you don't have to relearn it endlessly. Information is changed to make it compatible with the way your memory works, and so learning it is easy and efficient, saving you time in the long run and boosting your confidence and success. Well-learned information is there whenever you need it, wherever you are – and in a form in which it can be explored, organized and then produced in the most effective way.

So how do you make *any* kind of information memorable? There's a one-word answer to that: **IMAGINATION**.

The Emperor Napoleon once said that 'imagination rules the world'. We all have powerful imaginations, seen in dreams and fantasies, and used when we're reading books, listening to radio plays and working through problems.

It's imagination that allows us to take information and change it, to make it memorable. As long as you can return it to its original form when the time comes, it simply makes sense to explore and learn it in a form that your mind can handle.

It's time for a little imagination training. Below are four everyday words. Spend a few moments picturing each one in your imagination. In the first instance, simply try to imagine each object with as much clarity and in as much detail as possible.

- box
- tree
- car
- cake

Next, return to each item, and imagine picturing it from different angles. Can you imagine walking round it, seeing it from above, even getting inside it and looking out?

Now try adding some sense information. Imagine touching the item: what does it feel like? Is there any smell, sound or taste? Add as many details as you can to your imaginary pictures.

Next, practise making information unusual. Anything is possible in the imagination, so make each of your four images as unusual as possible. You could visualize the objects in a strange place, or doing odd things, or becoming very large or incredibly small. Exaggerate to make the images bizarre and memorable. These skills are vital when it comes to powerful learning and remembering. You take control of information in your imagination, make it visual and unusual, and give yourself a range of sense triggers.

Feelings are also important. To practise the skill of inventing emotional reactions to information, go back to the first word, *box*. You should already have a memorable image in your mind – but your task now is to imagine *destroying* it. How would you go about wrecking the box? What would your feelings be as you ripped it up, set fire to it or attacked it with a chain saw?

Next, imagine you're scared of the *tree*. How could you use your imagination to make this tree the most frightening thing in the world?

Turn the *car* into a source of hysterical fun. How could you picture it so that it made you roar with laughter?

Finally, invent an embarrassing moment involving the *cake*. Involve yourself in the action, and imagine the feeling of utter embarrassment.

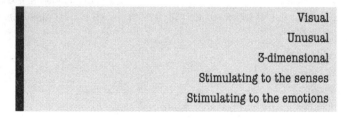

Visual
Unusual
3-dimensional
Stimulating to the senses
Stimulating to the emotions

As soon as a piece of information has been given these characteristics it can be connected with others in a memorable pattern. It's like inventing a story about your material.
Each item becomes one step in the story, prompting you to remember the next.

One item can transform into another, or explode and release the next image. You can imagine joining items together, putting one thing on top of another, or seeing an object come to life and do something bizarre and memorable to the next item on the list. Remember, anything is possible in imagination. The story doesn't have to have any real logic – only the connections you create.

To link these four words together in a story, you might imagine opening the box to find a tiny tree inside. You could take the tree and fix it to the rear view mirror in your car, and then drive off – straight into a giant cream cake sitting in the middle of the road.

- Think of the *box*, and you'll remember finding the *tree*.
- Think of the tree, and you'll recall fixing it in your *car*.
- Picture driving off in your car, and you'll remember how you felt when you smashed into the giant *cake*.

BOX → TREE → CAR → CAKE

However long a list is, you only need to deal with one item at a time. Make each link strong enough and it'll take you to the end of your story.

The structure of the brain

To help you appreciate just what your brain is capable of, let's take a look at how it's structured.

St Augustine said, 'People travel to wonder at the highest of mountains, at the huge waves of the sea, at the long courses of rivers, at the vast compass of the ocean, at the circular motion of the stars and they pass by themselves without wondering.'

Inside our heads we are wondrous indeed. In fact, the more we explore our amazing inner universe with all its range and its complexities, the more we realize there is to discover. There are three clearly defined areas of the brain:

1 *The Reptile brain*. Also known as the stem brain, it oversees the primitive survival mechanisms such as self-protection, reproduction, nourishment and shelter. It's also responsible for understanding physical reality, collected via the senses.

2 *The Mammalian brain*. This brain area represents a quantum leap in terms of evolutionary development. It's here that feelings, emotions, memories and experiences are assimilated. It's also the part of the brain that deals with bodily needs and functions such as hunger, thirst, sexual desire, body temperature, metabolism and immunity. Having collected a vast array of information via the senses and bodily sensations, it then passes that knowledge on to the largest part of the brain, the thinking part.

3 *The Cortex*. This part makes up around 80 per cent of the total brain. Here resides the intellect, where reasoning, decision making and linguistic ability result in purposeful voluntary actions. It's here too that many believe the sixth sense of intuition can be found. This is the part of us that is able to perceive information that is not picked up by our other senses. It's the superior qualities of the cortex that stand us apart from all other living things and make us unique as a species.

As well as this tripartite brain there's another division into the left and right hemispheres. These are responsible for the different modes of thinking, and they specialize in particular skills.

The left hemisphere. This works in a logical, rational, linear and sequential manner. It takes responsibility for such things as speech, writing, details, facts and organization.

The right hemisphere. This part of the brain works in a disorganized, random but more holistic way. It relies on intuition, and deals with feelings, emotions, visualization and aspects of creativity. Although each part of the brain has its own particular responsibilities, all the parts communicate and interact with each other. If we delve at a more microscopic level into how the brain works, it becomes even more fascinating.

There could be 100 billion neurons in your brain. These cells pass messages back and forth throughout the brain to the central nervous system. They're able to do this via electrical and chemical reactions. Under the microscope a neuron could be mistaken for a minute creature from the deep. It consists of a central body with feathery tentacles known as dendrites. The dendrites have attachments called synapses, where the exchange of chemical signals takes place. Once stimulated by a chemical signal, a dendrite sends an electrical impulse to the cell body. This triggers a larger electrical pulse onto the axon, which acts like a lightning conductor. It channels the signal at great speed through its length, and out to other cells in the brain. An outer coating of the fatty protein myelin helps enhance the speed at which the message travels. The final stage of the process occurs at the synapse, the junction between one neuron and another.

Neurons store information and act together to cause actions and reactions. They work in assemblies, each with specific tasks. Some deal with the outside world through the senses and movement, while others are responsible for internal communication between the areas of the brain to ensure we can think, imagine, create and be aware. These assemblies communicate with each other, simultaneously sending and receiving messages over great distances and at phenomenal speed, while also being aware of the needs of the whole body.

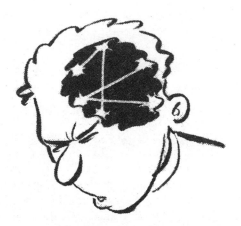

Each neuron can have thousands of connections to others. Add to that the fact that each cell can react or fire up around 500 times a second, and it's clear that the human brain is breathtaking, and its capabilities awesome.

Where memory fits in

Memory is complicated, to say the least. Most scientists now accept that memory is a set of systems operating in different parts of the brain. There are also different types of memory.

Procedural memory. This is the unconscious ability to do such things as run, drive a car, ride a bicycle, play a piano or juggle.

Semantic memory. This is where our knowledge of the world is stored. For example, it's your semantic memory that knows that kangaroos come from Australia and that Sydney has an amazingly designed opera house.

Episodic memory. This is the memory that records and stores past events, but is not always reliable. For example, your semantic memory might record facts about Australia, but you might not be able to remember all the details of a holiday you spent there.

Prospective memory. This is the system that lists the things you have to do in the future. It's one of the most unreliable of our memory systems.

So human memory is phenomenally complex – and yet the techniques for using it better and getting more out of it every day are remarkably simple.

Storytelling

Let's return to the list of words at the start of this chapter:

> chocolates, potatoes, soap, milk, paper towels, coconut, bananas, cheese, wine, bread

Here's an example of how an imaginary story could be created to turn each item into a memorable picture, and then to link each one to the next.

Imagine...

...opening a box of expensive chocolates, only to discover to your horror that each one has been replaced with a potato! You investigate further by starting to peel one of the potatoes, and you discover when you bite into it that it's made out of soap. You need to get the taste out of your mouth, so you take a long drink of milk, but unfortunately the carton has a leak, and the milk pours all over you, and out across the floor. More and more milk is pouring out, and you try to mop it up with some paper towels, but it's no good. The level is rising fast. Sitting on top of the towel rail is a coconut. As you watch, it grows and grows, until it's big enough for you to sit on and float on top of the milk. A banana floats by, and you fix it on to your coconut boat as a mast – then use a large triangular piece of cheese as a sail. You find a bottle of red wine on board, and use that to paint a colourful design on your sail. Unfortunately, though, you've been a bit rough and a number of holes have been torn in the sail – which you try to patch up with pieces of bread.

Read the story through again, trying to picture it all vividly. After that, see how many of the ten shopping list items you can remember. Simply go back through the story in your mind, link by link, and write down each item as it appears.

It began with a box of *chocolates*. Inside that were *potatoes*, which turned out to be made of *soap*. You tried to get rid of the terrible taste with *milk*, but the carton leaked and you used *paper towels* to mop it up – in vain. As the milk levels rose, you used the huge *coconut* as a boat, and fitted it with a *banana* mast and a *cheese* sail. You painted the sail with *wine*, tearing it in the process – and the story ended with you repairing the holes with pieces of *bread*.

It might help to imagine filming the strange events. Your mind's eye becomes a camera, able to zoom in on key details, move with the action, and explore everything that's going on. When you replay the mental film, you'll be able to recreate all the details of the story.

Put the technique into practice. Lay aside any other strategies or habits you might have picked up. Most important of all, be positive. Don't be tempted to think that the following list is too long to learn. You're only dealing with one item at a time, so it could be *any* length, and you'd still be able to remember it.

Bear in mind all the key points. As you go along, each item needs to be visualized, made unusual and memorable, and then connected vividly to the next. Abandon all normal logic, but make sure there's a strong reason for you to remember the next item on the list – and the stranger, more exciting, frightening, embarrassing, violent or funny the link is, the better. Exaggerate, and let your imagination run riot.

Here's the list: 20 everyday words. Take as much time as you need to transform the list into a memorable story, then play it back in your mind's eye and see how many of the words you can write down, in order. There's no reason why you can't even do the same thing in reverse. Simply follow the chain of events back to the start.

> television, clown, rabbit, fire, tea, pocket, scissors, snake, bin, castle, slide, bush, money, newspaper, ant, sandwich, ring, basin, coal, cat

Summary

Return to the adverts you explored at the start of this chapter. Do you have some clearer insights now into why they stuck in your brain – maybe for decades? It wasn't chance: they were designed to be memorable, just as you can design all the real information you want to learn and fix it in your mind.

Think about some of these key themes.

Imagery. How do you think the images were chosen, and why did they have such impact?

Structure. Were different bits of the advert held together by a story, song, or some other means?

Senses. Which of your senses were activated, and how?

Emotions. What reactions were the advertisers hoping for? Humour, surprise, nostalgia, desire...?

And when you've considered what the advertising agency did, think about what you did to make the memories last: visualize the images, put yourself in the picture, tell someone about the joke, whistle the jingle...

Many of these key aspects of memory will be central to the strategies and systems you learn during the rest of the week as your brain training gathers pace.

SUNDAY
MONDAY
TUESDAY
WEDNESDAY
THURSDAY
FRIDAY
SATURDAY

Quick-check

Try these questions to test your ability to learn a list of words: in this case, 15 office items. Give yourself five minutes to commit the words to memory, in order, using the techniques you've explored today; then cover them up and see how many of them you can recall. Answer all the questions before checking your success.

> photocopier, chair, coffee machine, bin, pen, telephone, computer, stapler, filing cabinet, shredder, paper-clip, calculator, desk, ruler, calendar

1. What is the third word on the list?
   a) computer ☐
   b) ruler ☐
   c) coffee machine ☐
   d) chair ☐

2. What comes between *computer* and *filing cabinet*?
   a) stapler ☐
   b) coffee machine ☐
   c) calendar ☐
   d) telephone ☐

3. Which word is after *paper-clip*?
   a) shredder ☐
   b) pen ☐
   c) chair ☐
   d) calculator ☐

4. What comes before *pen*?
   a) stapler ☐
   b) bin ☐
   c) desk ☐
   d) filing-cabinet ☐

5. Can you recall the tenth word?
   a) shredder ☐
   b) paper-clip ☐
   c) stapler ☐
   d) calendar ☐

6. Which word comes before *telephone*?
   a) bin ☐
   b) pen ☐
   c) coffee machine ☐
   d) computer ☐

7. What is between *desk* and *calendar*?
   a) shredder ☐
   b) chair ☐
   c) stapler ☐
   d) ruler ☐

8. What is the second item on the list?
   a) coffee machine ☐
   b) pen ☐
   c) desk ☐
   d) chair ☐

9. Which of these words is somewhere on the list?
   a) printer ☐
   b) photocopier ☐
   c) scanner ☐
   d) lamp ☐

10. What was the 11th word you saw?
    a) paper-clip ☐
    b) shredder ☐
    c) calculator ☐
    d) ruler ☐

TUESDAY

Think like a genius

It's very easy to get trapped into narrow ways of thinking, limiting the way you use your brain and preventing you from realizing your full potential. If memory feels hard and learning seems boring, if each mental challenge is just another struggle to overcome, if success means simply avoiding catastrophe... then something has gone badly wrong, and needs to change. You have to take a very different approach, but it's worth it. The benefits are fantastic.

Great learners enjoy what they do. They take an active approach, tackling each challenge in an energetic and entertaining way. Whatever the information they want to learn, they take control and mould it into a form that suits the way their memory works. And they're liberated in their thinking, bringing all their mental skills to bear. They're strategic and organized, so they save time and achieve real results; but they're also imaginative, they have fun with their learning, and they get much more out of the process than just remembering something. Their powerful approach to memory lets them engage with it more fully, understand it more deeply, and do really clever things with it as a result.

Global thinkers

Many of history's most famous thinkers and achievers have a key trait in common – the ability to use all of their brain.

   Thumbing through a book that explores the sketches of the artist Leonardo da Vinci, one is struck by his breadth of subject matter and inventiveness. He was not only a highly gifted artist, he was also an engineer and military expert, possessing a degree of curiosity and ingenuity that made him outstanding. Lewis Carroll made his living teaching mathematics at Oxford University, but he also tapped into the power of his imagination when he wrote *Alice's Adventures in Wonderland* and *Through the Looking Glass*. Albert Einstein – still one of the figureheads in the world of science – also explored the world of philosophy. He once said, 'Imagination is more important than knowledge. It is a preview of life's coming attractions.'
   What these exceptional men had in common was an approach to thinking that is described as *global*. As outlined in yesterday's chapter, as well as the brain being divided into three parts, reptile, mammalian and cortex, it's also divided into two sides, left and right. The left side is responsible for logical, rational, linear and sequential thought, while the right

side looks after the more intuitive, holistic, random side of our thinking.

Da Vinci, Carroll and Einstein did not just tap into one side of their brain, they capitalized on both. Although specialists in their fields, they widened the scope of their expertise, whether it was to paint sublime pictures and design flying machines, or work on the intricacies of mathematics while writing about a young girl walking through a mirror into another reality.

Although we all do tap into both sides of our brains, we tend to prefer to use one side or the other. We shy away from pushing out of our comfort zones to explore and practise ways of thinking we consider difficult. We're leaving so much brain power untapped.

A global approach means that the brain is being utilized fully. Learning becomes easier, more can be achieved, thresholds and limitations challenged. The saying, 'None of us is as good as all of us', could well be applied to how we approach using our brain's capabilities. What we need to do is to develop our right-brained modes of creative, intuitive thinking, as well as the left-brained skills of verbal and written communication, organizational and rational abilities – and, crucially, start putting the two sides to work *together*.

Global learning is further enhanced by using the senses and by immersing oneself in a subject. By diving in and becoming engrossed and asking the who? what? why? when? how? questions, understanding is enhanced and learning becomes even more effective.

The advantage of adopting this global approach is that it also produces positive emotions via increased brain power, and encourages us to be even more adventurous in our thinking.

More memory practice

Don't worry that you'll get confused between the different mental pictures you create and the stories you invent. Your memory is unbelievably powerful, and it's able to keep all the different batches of information separate.

Put this principle to the test by learning another list of words, and then checking that you can still remember the

20 words you learned at the end of the last chapter. Here's the new list of words:

> grass, elephant, computer, matchbox, mirror, football, rocket, biscuit, caravan, fence, spade, cow, tent, cloud, lamp, shorts, basket, train, sun, glass

Remember the key characteristics of memorable information. These words need to be visualized in as much colour and detail as possible, exaggerated and given sense and emotion triggers, then linked together into an unusual, connected story. Give yourself a maximum of ten minutes to commit this list to memory – to *make it memorable*. As soon as you've completed your story and checked that you can remember all 20 words, return to the first list, and read out *those* 20 words – beginning with *television*.

You now have 40 items committed to memory, in two distinct mental 'files'. As long as each story is built on strong links, they won't overlap or become confused. In each case, the first word is all you should need to start off the chain of images – and you'll find that you can recall the list backwards as well as forwards.

> Memory techniques like these may seem disordered and fanciful, but in fact they create a real sense of organization and precision.

Picture clues

So far you've worked with lists of objects, each of which provided a definite image. You know that you can memorize lists of shopping or presents, or all the items to be taken on holiday – but what about information that's harder to visualize? What happens when you need to remember words that suggest no obvious pictures?

The trick is to use *picture clues*. You think up a picture to remind you of your original information. It may well be very different from the actual word you're trying to learn, but it'll be enough to jog your memory. Picture clues can be based on how a word sounds, what it looks like, or on an image that it suggests. You can use any picture that works for you.

As an example, imagine you had to learn the following list:

> ### First ten U.S. presidents since World War Two
> Truman, Eisenhower, Kennedy, Johnson, Nixon, Ford, Carter, Reagan, Bush, Clinton

Here are some suggestions for picture clues but the best ones are always those that you think up yourself.

- *Truman*: perhaps a cricketer, like Freddie Truman, or someone taking a lie-detector test to prove that they're a 'true man'.
- *Eisenhower*: maybe you simply think of 'ice' – or it could be an 'ice shower'.
- *Kennedy*: you could picture Barbie's boyfriend Ken, or maybe a rocket being launched from the Kennedy Space Centre.
- *Johnson*: the image here could be of Johnson's baby powder, or the actor Don Johnson.
- *Nixon*: perhaps a Nikon camera, or a thief 'nicking' something.
- *Ford*: a river-crossing or a Ford car.
- *Carter*: a man pulling a cart.
- *Reagan*: a ray gun.
- *Bush*: a bush.
- *Clinton*: Clint Eastwood perhaps.

Spend a few moments coming up with an image clue that works for you, for each of the ten presidents' names. Once you have your images, learning them is as easy as learning the items on a shopping list. Simply take each one in turn, connect it with the next, and build up a memorable story.

You might imagine...

SUNDAY MONDAY TUESDAY WEDNESDAY THURSDAY FRIDAY SATURDAY

...Freddie *Truman*, still wearing his cricket gear, climbing into an ice-cold shower – *Eisenhower* – only to find Barbie's plastic boyfriend Ken – *Kennedy* – in there already. Ken is covering himself with Johnson's baby powder – *Johnson* – before he poses for photographs taken using a top-of-the-range Nikon camera – *Nixon*. The photographer races off to get the pictures printed in his *Ford* car, but he's driving so fast that he crashes into a *Carter*. Enraged, the carter pulls out a ray gun – *Reagan* – and the poor photographer tries to hide in a nearby *Bush* but Clint Eastwood – *Clinton* – is already using it to hide from the Indians.

Whatever kind of story you create, run though it a few times in your mind, checking that you can remember all ten picture clues and that each one links clearly to the next.

When you're confident with your imaginary tale, use it to write down the names of the ten presidents from memory.

Check that you can still remember the two lists of 20 words – one began with *television*, the other with the word *grass* – and the ten-item shopping list. All the pieces of information should be there in their individual files: already that's 60 pieces of data memorized with ease.

Image illustrations

With practice, you'll get used to thinking of a picture to represent any kind of information. Often you don't need to worry about every last bit of the original material – just think of a picture that's going to jog your memory. After all, without these techniques you'd probably remember the information *eventually*. It's in there *somewhere* – you just need a prompt to retrieve it when you really need it.

Say you wanted to learn the following list of jobs to do in a day at work:

- Set a date for the office party
- Order new calendars
- Buy a present for Paul
- Arrange a game of squash
- Pay cheques in to the bank
- Book your holiday.

You might come up with the following image 'illustrations' for each job:

- The party itself, full of sounds, tastes and feelings
- A large, colourful calendar
- Paul, holding his present
- A squash racket
- Large cheques
- A sun-baked beach.

You could then connect the images into a story like this:

The office party is in full swing, and the noise is so great that all the calendars fall off the walls. One hits Paul as he's opening his present and he collapses, unconscious. You prod him with your squash racket to check he's OK, then write him a cheque for compensation, which he uses to pay for a holiday in the Caribbean.

If you ran through that chain of images a few times on your journey to work, you'd have a powerful memory story to help you organize your day. You could consult this mental checklist wherever you were, and make sure that all the key tasks were completed by the end of the day.

Numbers

So far we've concentrated on remembering words and phrases, but it's also possible to use the same basic techniques to memorize numbers.

These days, most of us don't need to remember large amounts of numerical information. What we need to get to grips with are PIN codes, burglar-alarm settings, addresses, extension numbers, birthdays, times – all mostly made up of just a few digits. Having a strategy for learning these small groups of numbers saves a great deal of time and trouble.

As with the lists you've learned so far, the trick is to think in pictures. You need to invest a little time deciding on a picture to represent each of the ten digits, 0–9, so that you always have an image clue to use.

On a blank piece of paper, jot down the ten digits, with enough space alongside each one to write a brief description – or make a quick sketch – of the image you give it.

You could base your images on what a digit looks like. In that case, you might draw a ball next to 0, or write 'sun' or 'orange'. Next to the number 1 you could write 'pen' or 'pencil', or draw a needle or pin. You just need to think of one key image for each digit.

You might base some of your images on what a digit sounds like, choosing something that rhymes with it: 2 could be 'shoe', 3 might become 'bee', 4 'door ' and so on.

Another possibility would be to make use of the significance a digit might already have. If you were born on the sixth day of the month, for example, you might illustrate 6 as a birthday present, or write 'birthday cake' on your piece of paper; 7 could become one of the Magnificent Seven; 8 an After Eight mint.

When you've come up with an image for each of the digits, check that no two are so alike that you'll get confused. You can also fine-tune your system as you use it, so don't be afraid to develop and improve your set of ten images.

Using this number system is simple. To learn a group of numbers, you just transform each digit into the image you've assigned it, then connect the images together into a scene or story. The one crucial extra step is to make the scene appropriate to your reason for learning the numbers in the first place.

For example, if the code to disarm your burglar alarm was 3264, then your number system might give you these four images:

You could imagine a huge honey-bee landing on your shoe. You try to flap it away with a birthday present you're holding, but the bee flies off and out of the house through the open front door.

Bee on *shoe*, threatened with *birthday present*, flying through *door* – this simple scene gives you the four important numbers: 3264.

The final step would be to connect this scene with your reason for learning the four numbers. You might imagine sounding the alarm as the bee escapes – to remind you that these images give you the code for the alarm.

Perhaps you want to remember that the PIN code on your bank card is 7205.

For 7 you might have an image of *heaven* (rhyme); 2 might be represented by a *swan* (shape); 0 could be a *football* (shape); 5 might turn into a *hook* (shape).

You might picture yourself standing in heaven, when you see a majestic swan. You climb onto its back, and enjoy flying – until you realize that people on the ground below are pelting you with footballs. To get your own back, you burst every one you can catch, using a large metal hook.

To connect this strange tale with the original numbers, you might imagine seeing an animated version of it on the screen of a familiar cash machine. Every time you use a machine for real, you'll remember the cartoon – and see yourself in *heaven*, climbing onto the *swan*, being pelted with *footballs* and bursting lots of them on a *hook*: your bank card PIN must be 7205.

Practise using your own number system by memorizing the following historical dates.

Step 1: *Turn each digit into the appropriate image.*
Step 2: *Connect the images into a short story.*
Step 3: *Connect the story with your reason for remembering.*

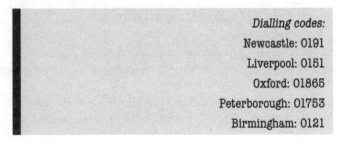

Dates:
Gunpowder Plot: 1605
Death of Ovid: 17
Battle of Waterloo: 1815
Henry VIII born: 1491
Ruin of Pompeii: 79

Below are five UK dialling codes. See how quickly you can use your system to commit them to memory – and remember you don't need to worry about the first two digits each time, because all STD codes begin with 01.

Dialling codes:
Newcastle: 0191
Liverpool: 0151
Oxford: 01865
Peterborough: 01753
Birmingham: 0121

Any kind of information can be given a picture clue, and those pictures can be linked into memorable stories. The information is simply being made compatible with the way human memory works.

Summary

To round off today, think about the implications of the skills you've learned. You've seen how to get your brain in gear and start learning lists of words; and what you can do to make numbers easier to recall. So how is that going to benefit you in real terms? What does this sort of memory training mean for your life, in work and out?

If you can learn lists, you can start organizing the practical tasks you want to achieve and take more control of your time and effort. You can remember directions, processes, targets, skills; the key points in documents or presentations; notes for meetings; priorities in negotiations. You can also make long-term plans, including less tangible ideals: skills you'd like to learn, experiences you want to have, aspects of your character you're working on, dreams you want to turn into realities.

With strategies for learning numbers you can fix vital details into your memory: times, dates, serial numbers, security codes, document references, financial projections... You can cope better with the facts and figures you need to know, but you can also choose new, ambitious ways to use and show off your memory skills.

Quick-check

Use the first five questions to practise remembering names.

You have three minutes to learn the following people. Don't worry about the order of names. You'll need to be able to match first names to surnames, so use the techniques you've been practising to commit them all to memory.

> Walter Black, Chrissie Webster, Eileen O'Reilly, Scott Gardener, Mike Rembrandt, Charlie Wu, Karen Baker, Len Windsor, Tina Strong, Ronnie Martinez

Now, from memory, fill in the missing names.

1. Eileen _____
   a) Black ☐
   b) Wu ☐
   c) Windsor ☐
   d) O'Reilly ☐

2. _____ Gardener
   a) Scott ☐
   b) Charlie ☐
   c) Mike ☐
   d) Ronnie ☐

3. _____ Rembrandt
   a) Mike ☐
   b) Scott ☐
   c) Chrissie ☐
   d) Ronnie ☐

4. Karen _____
   a) O'Reilly ☐
   b) Wu ☐
   c) Baker ☐
   d) Windsor ☐

5. _____ Strong
   a) Len ☐

   b) Walter ☐
   c) Tina ☐
   d) Scott ☐

Now test yourself on a sequence of numbers.

Give yourself three minutes to learn the following serial code, using the method you learned in this chapter.

▌ 9 4 8 3 7 1 0 9 2 7 5 8

Cover the numbers and answer these five questions:

6. What is the third number?
   a) 5 ☐
   b) 6 ☐
   c) 7 ☐
   d) 8 ☐

7. What comes before 0?
   a) 1 ☐
   b) 2 ☐
   c) 3 ☐
   d) 4 ☐

8. Which number comes after 3?
   a) 6 ☐
   b) 7 ☐
   c) 8 ☐
   d) 9 ☐

9. What is between 0 and 2?
   a) 6 ☐
   b) 7 ☐
   c) 8 ☐
   d) 9 ☐

10. Which of these numbers does not appear in the code?
   a) 5 ☐
   b) 6 ☐
   c) 7 ☐
   d) 8 ☐

WEDNESDAY

How to remember anything

You're approaching the halfway point in your week of memory training, so pause to consider any changes you've noticed already. Have you found any opportunities to use the memory techniques for real? By putting them to work you'll embed them in your learning and improve your thinking habits. The more they pay off, the more you'll want to hone your skills further.

Keep an eye out also for any of your existing strategies that work. Notice when you tie a knot in a handkerchief, go to a particular place to help you remember, run through the alphabet until one letter kick-starts your brain... Now you can also think about why these behaviours work, and what they tell you about your memory. If they work, keep doing them; otherwise, replace them with the tactics you learn as the week goes on.

And celebrate your successes. It's easy to underestimate the skill involved in scoring full marks on one of the memory tests, or the achievement of remembering things you've struggled with for years. Pat yourself on the back every time you prove you can use your memory well. Enjoy the learning challenges you're given – especially the things you now choose to do with your developing memory skills.

Recapping your learning

One of the best things about the sort of learning described in this book is that it cuts out wasted repetition. Once you've created pictures and stories to remind you of a set of information, you never have to start again from scratch.

You can quickly recap the material even if you haven't used it for months, simply by reminding yourself of the key images – and every time you do so you're strengthening the memories, rather than just learning the same material again.

Spend a few minutes now recapping some of the information you've learned so far in this book, the images and stories that allow you to recall:

- the ten-item shopping list, beginning with *chocolates*
- the list of 20 words beginning with *television*
- the list of 20 words beginning with *grass*
- the first ten U.S. presidents since World War Two
- the dates of:
  - the Gunpowder Plot
  - the death of Ovid
  - the Battle of Waterloo
  - the ruin of Pompeii
  - the birth of Henry VIII

- the dialling code for:
  - Newcastle
  - Liverpool
  - Oxford
  - Peterborough
  - Birmingham.

You're able to remember any kind of information by making it memorable, and so far you've learned more than 70 distinct pieces of information.

Practice makes perfect – so try memorizing the first ten numbers in Japanese. Don't be tempted to think that this is too difficult. The technique is one you're well used to by now. You simply invent an image-reminder for the way each number sounds, then link all ten together.

1	ichi	6	roku
2	nee	7	nana
3	san	8	hachi
4	she	9	q
5	go	10	ju

Image ideas:

1 and 2 – itchy knee
3 – sand
4 – sheep
5 – 'go' sign
6 – rock
7 – bananas
8 – a sneeze (it sounds like 'hatchoo!')
9 – a queue
10 – juice

Perhaps you imagine yourself...

...rubbing your itchy knee in the sand, when a flock of sheep rushes at you, knocking you flying across the beach. You try to get rid of the sheep by holding up a large sign saying 'Go', but it's no good: they're all settling down for the day on rocks by the shore, and opening up their picnic boxes – which are all full of bananas. Unfortunately, sheep must be allergic to bananas because they all start sneezing – 'hachi!' – and form a long queue at a stall selling juice, which they hope will wash away the offending taste.

> itchy... knee... san(d)... shee(p)... go... rock(u)... (ba)nana... hachi...
> q(ueue)... ju(ice)

Ten images, each jogging your memory about a Japanese number.

The best images and stories are always the ones that you think up yourself, so spend a few minutes putting your imagination to work on this list. Check it through a few times, reinforce or change difficult or confusing parts – then test yourself by covering up the list and reading all the numbers back from memory. If you were to recap your story a few times every day, within a week you'd know this list by heart.

The best-kept secret

Stories are powerful tools for giving otherwise abstract and unconnected pieces of information a memorable structure. But there is another strategy – one that has been called 'the best-kept secret' about your memory. It makes learning faster and easier, it works in the way your brain likes to work, and it has been used with incredible success for centuries.

Ancient Greek legend has it that super-rich Scopas threw a huge banquet, during which disaster struck. His banqueting hall collapsed on his hundreds of guests – among them Simonides, the poet, one of a handful of survivors. Identifying the bodies would have been impossible had it not been for Simonides' trained memory. By closing his eyes and mentally rebuilding the banqueting hall, he was able to connect every guest with their location in the room, and provide a perfect guest list and seating plan from memory.

This tale comes from a time when memory systems were taught and celebrated. How else could one teach, speak, argue cases of law or compose epic poetry without a practised ability to do it from memory? By Roman times, using mnemonic strategies came as second nature to great orators such as Cicero, who is known to have addressed the senate for days on end from memory. Before they were taught what to remember, students were taught how to remember it – and the central element of every memory system was what has come to be known as the 'Roman Room' concept, or the 'Memory Palace'. Simonides used the framework of a banqueting hall to contain the information he needed to remember the guests, and you too can use the frameworks – buildings, golf courses, towns, walks – of your everyday life to store vast amounts of information in an incredibly usable way.

It's a natural tendency of the human brain to think spatially, and to connect abstract information with concrete places. Have you ever got to the top of the stairs and forgotten what you were coming up for? If you return to the spot where you were standing when you had the urge to go up, your memory may well kick back into action. Detectives often take eye witnesses back to the scene of a crime to help them remember exactly what they saw. If you listen to music as you drive around, it's likely you can recall where you were the last time a particular song or piece of music came on. The Roman Room technique capitalizes on this strong link between memory and location. It makes use of the fact that you already know from memory many hundreds of mental frameworks into which information can be slotted and stored.

The route system

Step 1. Pick a building you know well. This technique also works well when you use walks, car journeys – even golf courses – but it's easiest to start with a simple building: your home, where you work or perhaps a hotel you visit regularly.

Step 2. Divide this building into ten separate areas. It often helps to sketch a quick plan on a piece of paper. The areas could be rooms, particular features or whole floors – just however you think the building can best be divided into ten zones.

Step 3. Decide on a route, from Area 1 to Area 10. It's important that you're sure of the route, because you'll always take the same mental walk around this building. What would be the most logical way of getting from the first area to the last?

Step 4. Close your eyes and imagine moving along the route. Start by picturing yourself standing in Area 1. What can you see? What does this place smell like and sound like, and what details set it apart?

From there, visualize yourself moving to Area 2. Again, bring this zone to life in your mind's eye. Keep doing this, going from place to place and spending a few moments in each one, until you arrive at the end of your route.

Step 5. As a final check, see if you can imagine making the journey in reverse. This shouldn't be a problem: in real life you have no difficulty remembering the way out of your house or back home from work. It's just a good way of making sure that you're fully confident with this memory route.

When you've completed these five steps, you're ready to put your route to use. It's been time well spent: you'll be able to use this mental structure many times, to help you remember many different types of information.

To use a route, you simply locate a different piece of imagery in each of the ten areas. These are exactly the same sort of image clues used to remember words, names, ideas or numbers. The route system just removes the need for a story to link them together; instead, the connecting structure is already decided upon. All you have to do is slot in the images.

Use your imagination to fix each image in place as powerfully as possible. As you make the mental journey around this building, think of unusual, funny, violent, memorable ways of placing an image into each room.

As an example, here's a sample route around a typical house:

1 front porch
2 hallway
3 living-room
4 dining-room
5 kitchen
6 laundry
7 staircase
8 bathroom
9 bedroom
10 study

If you were using this route to memorize a shopping list – apples, coffee, cakes, butter, sugar, oranges, mineral water, salt, treacle, cereal – you could imagine...

...stepping into the front porch, and finding a huge *apple* filling the room. You have to squeeze past it to get into the hallway, which is flooded with hot *coffee*. Imagine the smell, and the feeling of the hot liquid as you paddle out into the living-room. Here, all the furniture is made out of *cake*: a cake sofa, cake dresser – even a cake TV. You walk into the dining-room, where a meal has been set out on the table – but the only thing on every single plate is a block of *butter* – hardly a balanced meal! In the kitchen, every cupboard, tin and pan is full of *sugar*. Imagine opening up a high cupboard, and being showered with an avalanche of sugar.

The next area on this route is the laundry. Here, *orange-trees* are growing amongst the clean clothes – and the whole room is painted bright orange. The staircase has been turned into a cascading waterfall – but a very expensive one, using gallons of *mineral water*. There are three rooms upstairs. In the bathroom, the bath is full to the brim with *salt*. Imagine what it would feel like to take a bath here – and how it would taste if you accidentally got a mouthful! Lying down in the bedroom is just as uncomfortable, because someone has spilled sticky *treacle* all over the bedclothes. Your journey ends in the study, where the books on the huge bookcase have been removed – and replaced with packets of *cereal*. There's cereal all over the carpet, and the desk – it's even got into the expensive computer.

In practice, filling up a route like this is extremely fast. Once you've done it a few times, you'll be able to imagine moving from room to room with ease, and take just a few seconds to visualize fixing each image in place. Try it, and you'll find that retrieving the images is almost unbelievably easy.

DID YOU REMEMBER THE APPLES DEAR?

In the example route, you'd instantly remember:
- the apple blocking the porch
- the coffee flooding the hallway

- the cake furniture decorating the living-room
- the butter served up in the dining-room
- the sugar filling the kitchen
- the oranges growing in the laundry
- the mineral water cascading down the staircase
- the salt filling the bath
- the treacle spilled in the bedroom
- the cereal all around the study.

Design a route of your own. Follow Steps 1 to 5, then put your framework to use straight away to learn the following list of items to pack for an imaginary holiday.

> sunglasses, suncream, swimming costume, passport, travellers' cheques, camera, sandals, maps, tennis racket, toothbrush

It's useful to have several routes organized in your mind, so that you can use them in rotation. Once used, you'll find that the images have disappeared from each route by the time you come to use it again. On the other hand, you can fill a route with information of lasting value to you, recap it every so often, and retain it as a permanent resource.

Take time now to design a second route. Make it memorable, different from the first, but follow the same five steps. When you're confident of this second mental structure, practise using it by committing the following information to memory:

> *Bodies of the solar system, in order from the Sun:*
>
> 1 Sun
> 2 Mercury
> 3 Venus
> 4 Earth
> 5 Mars
> 6 Jupiter
> 7 Saturn
> 8 Uranus
> 9 Neptune
> 10 Pluto (now 'downgraded' to a dwarf planet, but still worth knowing about!)

As with the lists of U.S. presidents and Japanese numbers, you first need to come up with an image clue for each of these heavenly bodies. Here are some suggestions, but feel free to think up your own:

1 Sun – your son, or the *Sun* newspaper
2 Mercury – a thermometer
3 Venus – goddess of love
4 Earth – a pile of muddy earth
5 Mars – a Mars bar
6 Jupiter – perhaps a duplicator, or a 'dew pit'
7 Saturn – Satan
8 Uranus – uranium
9 Neptune – sea god
10 Pluto – Mickey Mouse's dog

Once you've got your ten image clues, you simply fix them into place around your route. Always be on the lookout for appropriate ways of slotting them into place, and try to make use of things already present in your mental structure – items of furniture, for example, as 'hooks' to hang them on.

If your second route was based on your workplace, for example, you might imagine pages from the *Sun* newspaper pasted across the window of your office; a thermometer fixed to the control panel in the lift; a pile of earth in the middle of the boardroom table, etc.

Give yourself enough time to fix each of the ten images in place, then see how quickly you can write them all down, in order, from memory. If you have trouble recalling any of them, simply leave a space and go on to the next area. It may take a little time to recall a few stubborn images, but all the clues are there somewhere.

When you're confident with this new data, spend a few minutes recapping the other information you've learned:

● the ten-item shopping-list, beginning with *chocolates*
● the list of 20 words, beginning with *television*
● the list of 20 words, beginning with *grass*
● the first ten U.S. presidents since World War Two
● the dates of:

- the Gunpowder Plot
- the death of Ovid
- the Battle of Waterloo
- the ruin of Pompeii
- the birth of Henry VIII
● the dialling codes for:
  - Newcastle
  - Liverpool
  - Oxford
  - Peterborough
  - Birmingham
● the first ten numbers in Japanese
● the ten items to take on holiday
● the ten items on the shopping list beginning with *apples*.

Along with the solar system list, that's 110 separate pieces of information, neatly arranged in mental files. Every time you recall them like this, you fix them even more firmly in your mind.

One of the most powerful benefits of the route system is that whole sets of information can be fixed into each mental space. This means that you could easily create a single route to hold details of all the projects you were working on, or all the jobs you wanted to get done in a given week, month or year. The route system gives you the power to be highly organized – but, within that framework, to be creative too, adding and removing images whenever necessary.

Memorizing sets of information

Using the 'house' route described earlier, here's an example of how *sets* of information can be included and memorized.

You might decide to make the front porch your 'staff training' room, if that was a key part of your work. You could decorate it with picture clues to remind you of:

● the outdoor activity course you need to book (rope swings and balance beams fitted around the porch)
● the names Judy and Roy, staff members you need to see about their appraisals (Judy might be performing a Punch and Judy show in a cupboard, and Roy could be sitting on the window-sill dressed as Rob Roy)

- the date 1st July, an important deadline (the digits to remember are 1 and 7, and this might give you the images paintbrush and heaven – so you could imagine using the paintbrush to create a dramatic illustration of heaven on the front door).

Whenever you return to the front porch in your mind, you'll find it filled with image clues for all the key details to remember about staff training. You can add new pictures when necessary, and remove those that are no longer required. To do that, either visualize the old images being removed or rubbed out, or simply stop highlighting them in your mind, and let them slip away naturally from your memory.

You might decide to make the bathroom your area for remembering details about the key tasks you need to accomplish before the end of the month. You could imagine:

- finding the bath full of old door signs (since you need to order new ones)
- flushing computer disks down the toilet (to remind you to replace a key software product)
- discovering Ben Hur using the shower to wash his golf clubs (to make sure you remember to organize a game of golf with your colleague Ben)
- seeing Ben Hur use his shoe to kick oranges around the bathroom (giving you the digits 2 (shoe) and 0 (orange), and thus a reminder to arrange the match for the 20th).

The mental routes you create can also help you read, digest and remember texts and documents. As you read, get used to breaking the information down into key points. You're going to be illustrating each point with an image clue – so what *are* the key points? How much detailed information do you need to retain, and what images would jog your memory about each main point?

As you're reading, jot down key words or phrases that would act as a sufficient 'crib sheet'. Reading a memo about a change of premises, for example, you might jot down:

- moving
- 5 December
- Derby

- 3 new jobs
- Paul in charge of project.

When you'd finished, you would give each point an image clue. Perhaps you imagine choosing slides to illustrate this information in a visual presentation. What picture would be appropriate for each idea?

You might choose:

- a removal van
- someone using a hook (5) to pull a nail (1) out of a shoe (2) – 5/12
- a Demolition Derby
- worker bees (3)
- the dome of St Paul's Cathedral.

Fixing the images into one of your memory routes, you might imagine:

- a removal van crashing into the porch
- a cobbler at work in the hallway, using his hook to prise a nail from a shoe
- a Demolition Derby taking place in the living-room
- three worker bees eating at the dining-room table
- the kitchen transformed into St Paul's Cathedral.

As always, the process written down looks more complicated than it is in practice. You could easily slot images into your route as you read through the text, and the habit of thinking in pictures is an easy one to pick up. Soon you'll be condensing all the material you read automatically, and coming up with memorable illustrations with ease.

Reading like this is almost certainly slower than you're used to – but how often have you 'read' a whole page without taking in a single piece of information? *Active* reading is much more focused, so it feels more tiring to begin with, but you do it in shorter bursts – and get out exactly what you put in. Give it a try, and soon you'll be reading not just for the sake of reading, but to understand and learn.

A newspaper article analysed a report about the things people liked least about their working life – and how they would go about making changes if they could. It broke the 'moans' and 'wishes' into two lists of ten key points – just as you could have done if you were presented with the entire research document.

To practise illustrating ideas picked out of larger texts, and fixing the images into a route, try coming up with a picture to represent each of the ten 'wishes' printed below, then arranging them around one of your mental frameworks.

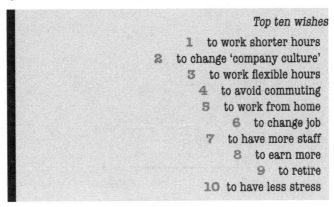

Top ten wishes

1   to work shorter hours
2   to change 'company culture'
3   to work flexible hours
4   to avoid commuting
5   to work from home
6   to change job
7   to have more staff
8   to earn more
9   to retire
10 to have less stress

Summary

Things you can do to back up your memory skills and establish yourself as an effective, active reader:

Preview a document or book, using the information on the cover, reviews, recommendations, and then skim-read to get a sense of what it's about. It really boosts your memory if things feel even a little familiar when you start to read, and this will also get you asking questions, drawing on prior knowledge and thinking about the best learning strategies to use.

Make notes while you're reading – either on the text itself, or in a notebook or laptop. Record your responses as much as the key ideas. Use colours, draw pictures, write questions – anything that helps you engage with and understand the text, and combine it with what you know. The notes will help you set up long-term memories of the important points, but keep the paper version too, as a handy memory-jogger.

Keep thinking about *why* you're reading something: for pleasure, to confirm your understanding, to learn new stuff... Set yourself a target, decide the level of detail you need and the amount of information to absorb, then choose memory strategies to match. Be sure to recoup your investment from every bit of reading you do.

SUNDAY

MONDAY

TUESDAY

WEDNESDAY

THURSDAY

FRIDAY

SATURDAY

Quick-check

These questions will challenge your ability to learn a list – of jobs you need to get done today. It's important to remember them in exactly the right order.

Study this list for three minutes, using the strategies you've learned so far to fix it in your memory.

1 Unlock safe
2 Call Andy French
3 Update website
4 Book meeting room for Tuesday
5 Order lunch
6 Meet Pippa Redwood at 3.45 p.m.
7 File receipts
8 Change printer cartridge
9 Finish writing report
10 Lock office

Make sure you can't see the list as you answer the following ten questions:

1. Who do you need to telephone?
a) Alice Andrews ❏
b) Andy French ❏
c) Frank Anderson ❏
d) Fiona Finch ❏

2. What should you file?
a) Invoices ❏
b) Letters ❏
c) Forms ❏
d) Receipts ❏

3. When do you need the meeting room?
a) Monday ❏
b) Tuesday ❏
c) Wednesday ❏
d) Thursday ❏

4. What should you do after making the phone call?
a) Book meeting room ❏
b) Update website ❏
c) Change printer cartridge ❏
d) Unlock safe ❏

5. What job comes before locking the office?
a) Finish report ❏
b) Change printer cartridge ❏
c) Order lunch ❏
d) Book meeting room ❏

6. Who are you meeting?
a) Pippa Redwood ❏
b) Paula Robinson ❏
c) Pauline Redmond ❏
d) Pat Rimmer ❏

7. What is the fifth job on the list?
a) Update website ❏
b) Finish writing report ❏
c) Lock office ❏
d) Order lunch ❏

8. What comes before the telephone call?
a) Change printer cartridge ❏
b) Update website ❏
c) Unlock office ❏
d) Order lunch ❏

9. What sort of task comes before ordering lunch?
a) Filing ❏
b) Telephoning ❏
c) Updating ❏
d) Booking ❏

10. What time is your meeting?
a) 3.30 ❏
b) 3.45 ❏
c) 4.15 ❏
d) 4.45 ❏

THURSDAY

Learning to learn

Have you stopped complaining about your bad memory yet? Too many people write off their memory skills, practically boasting about how poor they are. In the process they set themselves up for failure, missing even simple opportunities to help themselves and never exploring the practical strategies that could make all the difference. Of course, these same people are also constantly showing off the miraculous things their memories can do – but they only concentrate on the occasions when their brain lets them down. They make memory difficult and dull; but by now you should have seen the light and adopted a much more positive approach.

Memory training is a lifelong process. As a child you were able to do some of it really well, but you still had a lot to learn. As an adult, there are things that might have become tricky, but you also have many advantages in the level of mental maturity you've achieved. Some techniques in this book will prove their worth straight away, others may well take a while but keep trying, keep experimenting, keep thinking about the best ways to make them work for you. And don't give up if the going gets a bit tough. Nothing worth doing was ever completely straightforward.

Preparing for success

You have a test approaching, your emotions are in a turmoil as you realize you have just so much to remember. Your mind appears blank as you spin into panic. There's an important presentation looming, you feel stressed and anxious, convinced you will forget everything and make a fool of yourself. The radio interview that will give you the opportunity to talk about your company and its work is tomorrow, but how will you remember your name, let alone get your message across? Such responses are typical: we've all had that sinking feeling. Somehow it seems that whatever it was we did know has been lost in the recesses of our brain.

However it doesn't have to be that way. If you begin to put the following advice into practice and do the necessary preparation, you'll be putting yourself in the best possible setting to meet with success. It's good to know that by regularly using these tips and techniques you can enhance your ability to learn, remember with ease, get those answers right, interview with high impact and make a memorable presentation without reading from copious notes.

Step 1: put yourself in the best learning environment for you.
There's little point struggling to learn effectively if where you're working is too noisy, too quiet, too hot or too cold, too untidy or too bare and unwelcoming. Whatever is best for you, try to create it before you start to tackle whatever it is you have to learn and remember. The colour of the room you're in, the

music you might be playing, the smells you're inhaling, the pictures on the walls, even how you're sitting, can all have a profound impact on your emotions and therefore your attitude to your work.

Step 2: ensure you're in a positive frame of mind.

Feeling good about yourself and your abilities and anticipating a good outcome to your endeavours is very important. Just as no athlete worth their salt would dream of approaching the starting blocks of a race with a negative mindset, so you should see a successful outcome to your work. Recognize negative self-talk and replace it with something more constructive and positive.

You might find using creative visualization techniques could help you here. This is a method of relaxing and mentally creating a positive outcome to whatever it is you're about to embark on. It's a way of setting yourself up for success, not failure.

Other techniques include using affirmations. This is a method of repeating positive statements about yourself and your abilities. There's also the reframing technique. Here you choose to banish negative self-talk and select the positive way of viewing something.

Remember everything has a positive aspect to it if you really look hard enough. Choose to view your abilities and your approach to learning in a new way.

Step 3: see what's in it for you.

Now that may be easier said than done, especially if you have to deal with information that does not exactly excite you. But whatever you're tackling, you're much more likely to remember it if you can see how it will help you. In this way you become an active, not a passive, learner. Remember, there's a positive gain in everything, if you're prepared to look for it.

Step 4: be prepared to relearn.

We're creatures of habit in the way we think, and so we can limit ourselves by the mental boundaries we've set ourselves as a result of past experiences. Reframing, thinking outside the box, accepting there might be other ways of approaching a subject, and seeing the big picture, all help to encourage a more proactive stance to learning and retaining information.

Remember, too, the importance of the global approach to learning that we covered in the previous chapter.

Step 5: be courageous and don't be defeated by past mistakes or learning problems that seem insurmountable.

It could be the case that the way you were taught in the past didn't suit you, but you can do something about that now by knowing and using a wider range of learning styles. It's all too easy to stay in one's comfort zone rather than going out and trying new ways of learning and trying new ways of learning. Don't limit yourself or subscribe to the 'Better the devil you know' mentality.

Step 6: celebrate your successes.

Realizing how much you already know can really boost your confidence. Be willing to look back at past successes to see how far you've come already. Why not make a list of what you've achieved so far? Keep a notebook that celebrates your achievements; stick up pictures, photographs, certificates, anything that's a reminder of positive learning experiences.

Step 7: keep yourself in tip-top condition by eating and sleeping well and taking regular exercise.

A balanced healthy eating programme not only helps prevent unnecessary wear and tear on your body, it also energizes you and helps you keep mentally fit. Getting enough good-quality sleep should also figure in helping you operate at your optimum level. If you're not sleeping well, consider how you can relax and let go before going to bed.

Do you need to invest in a new mattress? Would using essential oils on your pillow help? or playing relaxing music? or using ear plugs? Also try to ensure you're taking regular exercise, at least twice a week. Sometimes just getting up a little earlier for a brisk walk can help set you up for a more energetic and positive day, and certainly after a day full of pressure, exercise helps to burn off excess stress.

So how can you begin to take action to ensure you incorporate this advice into your everyday life so that you're in the best possible frame of mind to learn and remember? List these questions in a notebook and next to each one jot down what action you need to take to improve things.

1 Are you in the best learning environment? What changes can you make?
2 Do you have a positive mental attitude? What improvements can you make?
3 How can you get the most out of any learning experience? What's in it for you?

4 What mental barriers have you set up? Identify a limitation around learning or memory that you have imposed on yourself. Where has it come from? How can you change it?

5 What is your preferred learning style? How could you improve your abilities in the other modalities? Mentally revisit a mistake or failure. How can you now regard it in a more positive way?

6 List five recent successes in order to appreciate your abilities. List five more you want to achieve.

7 How can you improve your diet? How can you improve your exercise regime? Are you getting good-quality sleep? Are you taking time for relaxation?

Recapping your learning

To conclude today, let's see how well you've remembered the lists from previous days.

What are:

- the ten-item shopping-list, beginning with *chocolates*
- the list of 20 words, beginning with *television*
- the list of 20 words, beginning with *grass*
- the first ten U.S. presidents since World War Two
- the dates of:
  - the Gunpowder Plot
  - the death of Ovid
  - the Battle of Waterloo
  - the ruin of Pompeii
  - the birth of Henry VIII
- the dialling codes for:
  - Newcastle
  - Liverpool
  - Oxford
  - Peterborough
  - Birmingham
- the first ten numbers in Japanese
- the ten items to take on holiday
- the ten items on the shopping list, beginning with *apples*
- the top ten 'wishes'?

Summary

Think about the role that other people play in your ongoing memory training. It's not always positive. Are you still being held back by things that people have said about you as a learner, maybe in the dim and distant past? Do you work or live with people who give you negative messages about your memory now? You may need to reprocess some of those ideas, old and new, and find ways to turn down the volume on any negative noises you hear. Maybe there are also issues with the way people give you information, or the conditions in which they expect you to learn. Don't let poor practice by others hold you back.

On the positive side, make the most of people who can help you improve. Which people inspire you to use your brain brilliantly? Who could you work with to strengthen your learning skills? It's also worth thinking about the people you're doing this for, because an improved memory won't just be good for you. Who will you impress, support, inspire? How might your new memory confidence change things for the better at work or in your home? You can be more organized, creative, accurate, efficient... and those benefits can quickly rub off on the people close by.

SUNDAY
MONDAY
TUESDAY
WEDNESDAY
THURSDAY
FRIDAY
SATURDAY

Quick-check

Here's a mixed set of questions, requiring you to use techniques you've learned during the week so far.

For the first three, give yourself three minutes to learn this set of words, in order.

> finance, leadership, mentor, portfolio, committee, stock, brochure, charity, holiday, contract

1. What is the fourth word on the list?
a) stock ❏
b) brochure ❏
c) portfolio ❏
d) finance ❏

2. What comes between *committee* and *brochure*?
a) stock ❏
b) finance ❏
c) mentor ❏
d) charity ❏

3. Which of these words is not on the list?
a) contract ❏
b) holiday ❏
c) leadership ❏
d) secretary ❏

To answer the next three questions you'll need to learn another list: this time, countries, and once again in perfect order. Give yourself three minutes.

> United States, France, Spain, Italy, Greece, Turkey, Kenya, Australia, Germany, Sweden

4. Which country is between Kenya and Germany on this list?
a) France ❏
b) Australia ❏
c) Spain ❏
d) Italy ❏

5. What is the last country on the list?
a) Germany ❏
b) Sweden ❏
c) France ❏
d) Spain ❏

6. Which of these countries is not on the list?
a) Portugal ❏
b) Turkey ❏
c) Greece ❏
d) United States ❏

For the final four questions, study this numerical information carefully. You've got four minutes to fix these facts in your brain.

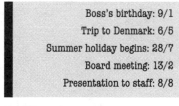

> Boss's birthday: 9/1
> Trip to Denmark: 6/5
> Summer holiday begins: 28/7
> Board meeting: 13/2
> Presentation to staff: 8/8

7. When does your summer holiday begin?
a) 26/6 ❏
b) 27/8 ❏
c) 28/7 ❏
d) 29/6 ❏

8. What is the date of the board
   meeting?
   a) 6/5 ☐
   b) 9/1 ☐
   c) 13/9 ☐
   d) 13/2 ☐

9. What's happening on 8/8?
   a) Training course ☐
   b) Presentation to staff ☐
   c) Office party ☐
   d) Trip to Denmark ☐

10. When is your boss's birthday?
    a) 15/6 ☐
    b) 3/8 ☐
    c) 9/1 ☐
    d) 11/12 ☐

SUNDAY

MONDAY

TUESDAY

WEDNESDAY

THURSDAY

FRIDAY

SATURDAY

FRIDAY

People skills

So much of the information we juggle these days, at work and at home, is about people. Computers and phones bring us into closer contact with other people than ever before, we know more about them, want them to know more about us, and we're constantly challenged to process names, numbers, jobs, addresses, birthdays, partners, likes, dislikes... for individuals, and amongst groups of interconnected colleagues and friends.

Personal information is particularly hard to handle because it's often communicated in an extremely unmemorable way. In noisy rooms, in the middle of other activities, out of context, late at night... You need a repertoire of robust memory skills to cope. But if you can, the benefits are great, allowing you to get so much more out of business events, social occasions, and just the daily interplay between all the people in your life, online and face to face.

Remembering names

One of the traditional party-pieces of the stage memory performer is remembering the names of every member of the audience. American magician and mnemonist Harry Lorayne made it his trademark, reciting theatrefuls of names night after night.

Many great military leaders, politicians and businesspeople have demonstrated equally breathtaking abilities to remember names. And yet for most people, remembering even one new name at a time is too much.

Perhaps you know what this feels like: you're at a conference, talking to a colleague, when a recent acquaintance comes over to join them and it's up to you to introduce them to each other – and suddenly you cannot remember either of their names. But imagine the opposite effect. Think how powerful it would be to be able to put names to faces at meetings and parties; how effective to remember key facts about the people you do business with; and how useful to know enough about memory to make everyone you meet remember you.

Step 1 is to listen, to hear people's names when you're introduced to them. Slow the process down: practise asking people to repeat their name if you missed it. Give yourself time to take it in.

Step 2 is to be interested in every new name you hear. Ask where it comes from, what it means, how it's spelled.

Step 3 is to switch on your mind's eye and visualize the name. Spend a couple of seconds imagining what the name would look like written down, or how it might come out as a signature.

Step 4 is to think of picture clues. What images come into your head when you think of the name? You're only looking for image triggers, so you might pick just part of the name to turn into a picture – an object, place or animal. Perhaps you think of a well-known person who shares the name, or a friend or relative of yours. You're making a vital memory move – moving away from abstract names to images that are real, unusual, interesting, colourful and memorable.

As the pictures start to emerge, **Step 5** is to try to make some connection with the real person in front of you. Imagine them holding whatever image has occurred to you, standing in the place that came to mind, or turning into the famous person you thought of. Think of their name as *illustrating* them in some way, and use your imagination to connect them with the image clues their name suggests.

For example, if you meet John Butcher, his name might well suggest meat, knives, chopping boards, roast dinners. As you talk to him, picture him taking out a huge meat cleaver and chopping great hunks of meat. As always you can involve your senses, switching on every facet of your memory, fixing your new friend in your mind with some powerful memory joggers.

With practice you can carry out these five steps quickly, without them getting in the way of conversation, and learn to give yourself enough memory clues to negotiate a meeting or party. Afterwards, it's up to you how many of the new names you choose to remember permanently. You can invest time in rehearsing the most important names and adding extra details so that you remember them long into the future.

Here are some more examples of image clues:

Surnames

- Anderson: perhaps someone hiding in an Anderson air-raid shelter, wearing a gas-mask
- Shelley: covered in sea-shells

- Rowling: constantly performing forward rolls
- Jones: singing in the style of Tom Jones
- Cathcart: pulling a cart piled with cats

First names

- Leo: lion
- Kate: kite
- Mark: covered in dirty marks
- Mike: holding a microphone
- Donna: prima donna ballerina

Leo Shelley could be visualized roaring like a lion *and* covered with shells. Mike Rowling could be trying to talk into his microphone *and* do hundreds of forward rolls. The trick is to build up a set of images, using all the time at your disposal to add extra reminders.

Every new piece of information can also be given an image and added to the mental scene. You might picture Kate Jones flying a kite while singing Tom Jones songs – at the same time as working out on an exercise bike and reading a book – representing the two hobbies she's told you about. If you recalled an image of Donna Anderson dancing around her air-raid shelter – and talking to a man in a fig-leaf – you'd remember that her husband was called Adam.

Remember people's names a few times by using these techniques, and you'll soon find that you know them off by heart. The strange imagery fades away, and you'll have forgotten *why* you know them – you just *do*.

Don't worry about getting names wrong. There are plenty of jokes about people confusing mental images and making embarrassing gaffes, but in reality this rarely happens. Mnemonic techniques just give you extra chances for learning more names – and when you get in the habit of remembering, that feeling of confidence is often enough in itself to make you remember.

Printed below are ten names, along with an extra fact about each one. Learn them all by using one of your mental routes. Think up images to jog your memory about each first name, surname and personal fact, then fix them in the spaces around the route.

> Tom Bird: enjoys fishing
> Sheila Walker: comes from India
> Richard Welsh: works with computers
> Arnold Donald: has a wife called Jean
> Tracey Cole: keen tennis player
> Jane Webster: American
> Ronald Smith: enjoys cooking
> Tara Singh: accountant
> Shaun MacDuff: keen horse-rider
> Juan Domingo: married to Maria

To recover the information, simply retrace your steps, moving from room to room in your mind. Each area on the route should contain clues to three key pieces of information: first name, surname and personal detail.

When you're confident with the imagery you've created, see how much of this information you can write down from memory. You may not remember every single person you meet, but these techniques will certainly help you feel more confident about keeping track of the important ones.

Thinking creatively like this is also a good basis for creative conversations. If you get used to thinking in pictures from the first moment you meet someone, then you're in the perfect frame of mind to discuss ideas and possibilities, and to solve problems. You'll also be aware of what it takes for other people to remember *you*. Give them time to hear your name and take it in. When you're talking about yourself, try to speak in pictures and stories, suggesting images and emotional responses for them to latch on to.

It can only benefit you if people remember you, and even simple strategies like these can be more effective than the most expensive business card.

Communicating effectively from memory

Talks, interviews and presentations

What you've already learned about how the brain functions, and how we learn and remember best, can stand you in good stead when it comes to performing in the public arena. You can tailor-make your message to appeal to all of your audience by considering the following nine points.

1 Ensure you paint pictures with the words you use. Remember how the brain likes unusual, dramatic, exciting images. Make use of similes and metaphors.

2 Tap into the three modalities by giving your audience something to see, hear and do.

3 Include such information, and present it in such a way, that it will appeal to both the left and the right sides of the brain. Give your talk a logical structure, but fill it with creative ideas – and try to engage as many of your audience's senses as possible.

4 Put yourself in the shoes of your audience. Carry out some research. How do they think? Help them to make connections with things they already know in order to lead them into new territories, and if possible, personalize the messages you're sending them. Tap into what will move or influence them emotionally.

5 Know that the way you open and close your presentation is important in terms of the powerful images you create. People pay most attention at the beginning and end of an interview or presentation, so it's also crucial to ensure your audience doesn't lose interest in the middle of what you're saying. Pay special attention to how you structure that part. Again make use of images, paint pictures, tell a story, give your listeners something to see, hear and do. Make links and connections with what's already been said and signpost where you're taking them next.

6 Before you begin any presentation or interview, anticipate success by visualizing how it will be. See yourself being

well prepared, dynamic and interesting and being well received by your audience. See and feel how receptive and appreciative your audience is. Experience how great you'll feel as you pat yourself on the back! Now practise and rehearse to perfect your performance. Imagining is powerful but certainly not enough on its own.

7 Using the learning and memory techniques you've been introduced to in this book, you can now create your whole presentation mentally by organizing the key information in one of your chosen routes. Take along memory joggers by all means, but just think how impressive it will be to give your performance without once losing eye contact with your audience or fiddling with pages of notes. We are always impressed with those who show they know their subject so thoroughly that they speak without a script.

8 If you're going to use visual aids, remember to make them colourful and meaningful to give them impact. Use images and few words. Don't forget, 'a picture paints a thousand words'!

9 Remember the importance of positive self-talk. Cultivating a positive mental attitude not only transforms the way you feel about yourself, it also gives a new and powerful dimension to the way you appear to others. Energy and conviction are

qualities that make your audience sit up and listen. Don't forget: your best visual aid is you!

So what action can you now take to improve the impact you will have when you next give a talk, interview or presentation?

Checklist

1 How can you improve the language you use?
2 How can you tap into the three modalities?
3 How can you appeal to left- and right-brained thinkers?
4 How can you engage the senses of your listeners?
5 How can you empathize with their points of view, their needs and their emotions?
6 How can you open and close powerfully?
7 How can you keep them interested in the middle?
8 Can you visualize success?
9 Can you select the key points of your presentation, interview or talk and place those points in one of your mental routes or settings?
10 How can you improve your visual aids?
11 Finally, what positive messages can you send yourself about your abilities and skills as a presenter or interviewee?

Summary

You're now in a position to be able to think through every aspect of a talk or presentation. You've got the strategies you need to communicate your message from memory, and you know how to make your audience remember what you say.

Think about memory as soon as you start planning your speech. Turn your key points into a list, choose an image for each idea and then connect the images into a memorable story or place them around a route. Practise using these clues to give your performance from memory. Rehearse it out loud, but also use your powers of visualization to see yourself in action, speaking with confidence and flair.

The real benefits will be clear when you do it for real. You'll be fluent and flexible, able to talk to time, answer questions, make eye contact, and never again worry about losing your notes or having your computer presentation break down. You'll also be presenting an organized argument, talking in pictures, being funny, interesting, believable... and so using your understanding of memory to activate all the other memories in the room.

SUNDAY   MONDAY   TUESDAY   WEDNESDAY   THURSDAY   FRIDAY   SATURDAY

Quick-check

Here are ten questions to help you practise your memory for names. Learn the following ten people, in exactly the order they appear here. This is the order in which they're due to speak at tomorrow's conference, and it will be your job to introduce them.

> Simon McDonald, Lou Chesterfield, Will Sharp, Katie Douglas, Angela Mann, Kevin Brown, Phil Downing, Wendy Lee, Gavin Shah, Harry Dale

1. Who's the first person on the list?
   a) Kevin Brown ☐
   b) Katie Douglas ☐
   c) Simon McDonald ☐
   d) Lou Chesterfield ☐

2. Who is due to speak immediately before Katie Douglas?
   a) Will Sharp ☐
   b) Wendy Lee ☐
   c) Harry Dale ☐
   d) Gavin Shah ☐

3. Who comes after Wendy Lee?
   a) Simon McDonald ☐
   b) Katie Douglas ☐
   c) Will Sharp ☐
   d) Gavin Shah ☐

4. Who will speak between Katie Douglas and Kevin Brown?
   a) Harry Dale ☐
   b) Wendy Lee ☐
   c) Angela Mann ☐
   d) Simon McDonald ☐

5. What is Mr Downing's first name?
   a) Paul ☐
   b) Phil ☐
   c) Peter ☐
   d) Perry ☐

6. Who is eighth on the list?
   a) Wendy Lee ☐
   b) Katie Douglas ☐
   c) Kevin Brown ☐
   d) Angela Mann ☐

7. What is the final speaker called?
   a) Kevin Brown ☐
   b) Angela Mann ☐
   c) Harry Dale ☐
   d) Simon McDonald ☐

8. What is Lou's second name?
   a) Chipperfield ☐
   b) Chesterton ☐
   c) Chesterfield ☐
   d) Champion ☐

9. Who will speak after Angela Mann?
   a) Kevin Brown ☐
   b) Will Sharp ☐
   c) Gavin Shah ☐
   d) Wendy Lee ☐

10. How many of the first names on this list begin with the letter K?
    a) 1 ☐
    b) 2 ☐
    c) 3 ☐
    d) 4 ☐

SATURDAY

Lifelong learning: your personal memory improvement plan

At the end of your week of training, remind yourself of the goals you set yourself earlier. Look back at the answers you gave at the end of Sunday. Can you now see the way forward – the way you'll start moving your memory skills in the right direction, changing the way you feel, and achieving what you want in each of the key areas of learning? Maybe you've already seen some real benefits from the work you've been putting in. Now is the time to plan properly for the future, to make sure these gains continue and you get the most out of your growing confidence and strengthening skills.

To start today, spend a moment looking at yourself. Produce a mental picture of yourself now, beginning to use these techniques every day, at work and in your life outside. In your mind's eye, watch yourself gaining real benefits from your memory training and starting to find new ways to make them work. And as you do so, think about how you're going to keep this momentum going and turn the improvements you've already made this week into a life's work. This is the last day of this book, but just the beginning of your real-life memory training.

Becoming a lifelong learner

The term 'lifelong learning' seems to be on everybody's lips these days. However, it's something that has always been practised by high achievers and those who have become great and inspiring role models over the centuries. Such people have naturally high curiosity and great enthusiasm for knowledge. They automatically keep their minds stimulated, challenged and exercised, as we saw earlier with the likes of da Vinci, Carroll and Einstein.

The very fact that you've bought and read this book puts you in the category of lifelong learning already. To continue the process, here are some suggestions.

See the advantages

As a result of committing to lifelong learning, you're likely to:

- continue to build and maintain high self-esteem
- stretch your mental muscles

- push out of your comfort zone and explore exciting new realms of knowledge
- develop new skills
- keep fresh, stimulated and motivated
- create and sustain a positive learning energy cycle
- improve your knowledge
- improve your earning potential
- become more creative
- use more of your brain
- feel more excited by life and all it has to offer.

How to do it

How can you ensure that lifelong learning becomes part of your everyday existence?

- Create the space to learn. Make use of travelling or waiting time to gain new knowledge. Get up a little earlier than usual and combine jogging with an MP3 player or an exercise bike with a book!
- Read in the bath and in bed. Turn the television off more often.
- Sign up for some classes, or another professional qualification. There's so much on offer these days. Learning with others can be stimulating and fun.
- Identify the need. What could you learn that will give added benefit to the work you do or the quality of your life?
- Is your learning environment as beneficial as it could be?
- Could you create a space where you know you'll be in the best possible atmosphere to learn? Remember, too, that you will have a preferred time of day for learning, and that the short intense burst approach might be better for you than taking huge chunks of time for studying.
- Try to immerse yourself in your chosen subject or subjects. Be wide and deep in your approach. Be aware of how much you already know – and build on it
- Check out your health. Do you need to make changes in your diet? Are you fit? Do you need a routine medical check? Are you sleeping well?

- Are you using your preferred learning style? Make sure you're absorbing new information in the way that's most beneficial to you. At the same time, try to build your strengths in the other modalities to enhance the global approach.
- Always try to use both sides of your brain to capitalize on global learning. Be logical, but give your imagination all the licence it needs.
- Keep hold of a positive mental attitude and don't put yourself down when you make mistakes. Be enthusiastic and excited by the rich process of boosting your memory and improving your knowledge and skills.

Tips for retrieving stubborn memories

Work has been done to highlight strategies for improving the recall of eye-witnesses to crimes – and it reveals tips for retrieving stubborn memories. There are four key points:

1 *Recreate the initial conditions*
   Witnesses to crimes or accidents are often asked to try to remember exactly what the weather was like.

How warm did the air feel? Was it windy? They also try to bring back their own feelings. Were they hungry or thirsty, sad or happy, excited or bored, on the day the incident occurred?

This is also useful when you're trying to recall images from a memory story or route. Try to tap into general memories, and to recall feelings, and you may well recover the precise images you're looking for.

2 *Concentrate on details, no matter how unimportant they seem*
We've seen that the brain works on a pattern of interconnections, and that information needs to be patterned and connected to suit it. It follows then that any details you remember can be used as a starting point, to begin a chain of associations back to the detail you're trying to recall.

If, for example, you return to an area on one of your mental routes and remember a detail that seems unimportant to the main image you're looking for, it's still worth concentrating on it and seeing what it yields. It could suggest something else; that might link to another thought – and suddenly the key image appears.

3 *Visualize a remembered scene from another point-of-view*
Witnesses to bank robberies might be asked to imagine what the robbers must have seen – and you can use the same principle to boost your recall. Get used to visualizing a mental route, story or scene from different angles, and letting your mind's eye search out the detail you're missing.

4 *Replay a memory in reverse*
After road accidents, eye-witnesses are sometimes asked to replay the events backwards: visualize the crashed cars... then describe what happened just before the crash... and what led to *that*...

It's a particularly useful strategy when you're trying to remember by using a story or route. If it doesn't work perfectly one way, try recalling it in reverse.

Your personal action plan

No matter how much you read about a subject, or how inspired you become, the only way to make any knowledge work for you in a purposeful way is to actually put it into practice.

You've already discovered that by using some of the exercises in this book. You've been able to remember nearly 200 things so far. There's nothing like doing something for it to have impact. All too often though, after finishing a course or a book, we put the written material away on a shelf and carry on as before.

That's why preparing a personal action plan is such a good idea. Give yourself written goals and timelines, put your plan somewhere where you'll see it regularly, and you'll be far more likely to take and *sustain* action.

Select from the following as guidelines, adding more if you need to, then lay out the information to suit you. For example, when considering 'Continue lifelong learning', you might have several topics or areas that you want to tackle under the **How?** heading, with a number of timelines under **When?**

What? How? When?

● Become a more positive thinker	● Adopt a global approach
● Continue lifelong learning	● Move out of comfort zones
● Acknowledge recent successes	● Obtain optimum health
● Find time	● See the advantages
● Knock down mental barriers	● Reward yourself
● Pamper yourself	● Practise and review
● Develop your imagination	● Memorize useful facts
● Memorize useful numbers	● Develop new routes for remembering

Tests

You should now feel confident about your memory, and aware of what you have to do to make it work. The basic principles are simple, and the applications are endless.

Give the information you have to learn:

- imagery
- emotional triggers
- exaggeration
- pattern.

Anything can be made compatible with the way your memory works, and represented as a set of linked pictures: jobs, names, times, dates, facts, presentations, interview answers, memos, reports. In the right form, your brain can hold unlimited amounts of data.

To confirm the progress you've made since starting this book, take part in this final set of tests. Use any of the techniques you like, individually or in combination. You can make up similar tests yourself in the future to help keep your memory in trim.

Test 1: word list

Memorize the following list of words. Try to do it in less than five minutes, then check your success.

sword, handbag, curtain, custard, rake, bomb, trombone, shark, mountain, dragon, leaf, cafe, biscuit, CD, boot, comb, gate, ice, oven, camera

Test 2: job list

Learn this list of jobs. Again, give yourself a maximum of five minutes.

1 order new letterheads
2 take laptop to be repaired
3 arrange meeting with Kelly
4 cancel trip to India
5 go to bank
6 submit invoices
7 play squash
8 call Chris (ext. 263)
9 lunch with Andy
10 book holiday, starting 25 August

Test 3: numbers

Use your number system to memorize the following imaginary extension numbers. You have ten minutes.

Scott: 8305

Rita: 1876

James: 2236

Pam: 4907

Daniel: 9301

Test 4: names

Below is a list of ten people you'll be looking after at a conference. You have ten minutes to learn all their names, so that you can write out the entire list from memory.

Jack Braine, Holly Harper, Christian Attley, Ashley Verne, Debbie Green, Frank Shepherd, Ray Oates, Helmut Schreiber, Dougal MacMillan, Hattie Chandler

To finish the tests, see how much of the information you've learned throughout the book is still fresh in your mind.

- ten items on the shopping list beginning with *chocolates*
- 20 words on the list beginning with *television*
- 20 words on the list beginning with *grass*
- the first ten U.S. presidents since World War Two
- the dates of:
  - the Gunpowder Plot
  - the death of Ovid
  - the Battle of Waterloo
  - the ruin of Pompeii
  - the birth of Henry VIII
- the dialling codes for:
  - Newcastle
  - Liverpool
  - Oxford
  - Peterborough
  - Birmingham
- the first ten numbers in Japanese

- the ten items to take on holiday
- the ten items on the shopping-list, beginning with *apples*
- the top ten wishes of workers in the research document.

That's a lot of information – and it's still just a glimpse of your memory's infinite power.

Remember:

1   It's important to understand how you learn best.
    What's your preferred learning style? Are you a left- or right-brained thinker?
    Do what you do well, but try to harness the full range of your learning possibilities.
2   You need to organize your learning.
    Look for the easiest ways to arrange the information you have to learn.
    Organize your approach to learning to make the process smooth, quick and fun.
3   You should tap into your imagination.
    Children have a naturally fertile imagination and so can you.
4   Adopt the best mental attitude.
    Be positive. Break bad thinking habits, motivate yourself, reward and encourage yourself.
5   Find the right learning environment.
    What surroundings will encourage you to be at your most receptive?
6   Match your healthy mind with a healthy body.
    Eat well, exercise regularly and get a good night's sleep.
7   You're never too old to learn.
    Don't be tempted to use age as an excuse for not continuing to learn and remember. You have more brain cells than you need, however old you are.
8   Practise.
    Do it! Start using the techniques you've learned in this book, and they'll soon become second nature.
9   Be a lifelong learner.
    Keep your brain stimulated and use it to go further in everything you do.
10 Your brain is amazing.
    Never underestimate your learning power. Its potential for storage and creativity is immeasurable.

Summary

You've done lots of very specific, strategic learning this week, and you know how to choose the best techniques for every challenge. But what about some of the knock-on benefits? Will your training have an impact on other, less 'directed' areas of your memory?

In the coming months, notice any improvements in your 'natural' memory: your instinctive recall, your ability to find the right word, the ease with which you connect with moments from the past. See if your short-term memory improves, for ideas, names, conversations. Are you making fewer slip-ups, avoiding confusion, finding that fewer things get caught 'on the tip of your tongue'?

Explore moments from your distant past. Are they any clearer, now you're more aware of using your senses and following connections?

And do you have clearer ideas about your future? When you think about the things you want to achieve, see if you're creating more vivid 'memories' of future successes – because your brain is simply better at forming ideas and exploring them in detail.

Try to recognize everything that changes for the better. As well as tangible improvements at work and beyond, celebrate the less obvious but equally important developments to your memory as a whole.

Keep up the good work and enjoy this new relationship with your amazing brain.

SUNDAY
MONDAY
TUESDAY
WEDNESDAY
THURSDAY
FRIDAY
SATURDAY

Quick-check

Use this set of questions to gauge the progress you've made this week.

1. How much confidence do you have now in the strength of your memory?
   a) None ☐
   b) Some ☐
   c) Quite a lot ☐
   d) A great deal ☐

2. What is the likelihood of you remembering the name of someone you met last month?
   a) Impossible ☐
   b) Unlikely ☐
   c) Likely ☐
   d) Certain ☐

3. How organized are you about all the jobs you need to remember?
   a) Not at all ☐
   b) Fairly ☐
   c) Very ☐
   d) Completely ☐

4. Which of these skills needs the most practice now?
   a) Learning lists ☐
   b) Remembering names ☐
   c) Recalling numbers ☐
   d) Memorizing speeches ☐

5. When you read a document, how much of it can you remember the next day?
   a) None ☐
   b) Some ☐
   c) Most ☐
   d) All ☐

6. Which area of your memory improvement has impressed you the most?
   a) The things I can learn ☐
   b) The techniques that work ☐
   c) The power of my brain ☐
   d) My capacity to keep improving from here ☐

7. How good are you at using imagination to strengthen your memory?
   a) Terrible ☐
   b) Not bad ☐
   c) Good ☐
   d) Brilliant ☐

8. How do you feel now about speaking from memory?
   a) Very nervous ☐
   b) Uncertain ☐
   c) Fairly confident ☐
   d) Assured ☐

9. Are other people likely to remember the things you do and say?
   a) Definitely not ☐
   b) Reasonably ☐
   c) Very ☐
   d) Completely ☐

10. How committed are you to being a lifelong learner?
    a) Not at all ☐
    b) Quite ☐
    c) Increasingly ☐
    d) Very ☐

Surviving in tough times

In difficult economic times, a confident memory is more important than ever – and your trained brain can be the difference between going under and coming out on top. Memory skills help you to work efficiently, adapt to change, and stay calm under the sort of pressure that so many of us are facing these days. This week, by boosting your concentration, enhancing your communication, and using your brain in new and exciting ways, you've equipped yourself with strategies that will set you apart from the competition. So, to finish, here are just ten of the ways you can make your memory work for you when it matters most.

1 Be confident

You no longer need to hope your memory will work, or worry about it letting you down. You know exactly how to make it do what you want – so now it's time to make the most of that confidence and search out ways to let your memory give you the edge. They say that attack is the best form of defence, and it's that spirit of pushing forward and tackling challenges head on that will give you the best chance of success. Just doing what you've always done isn't going to be enough any more. So be proactive, have the confidence to put your new memory skills into action, and see where they take you.

2 Stay cool

Cares and worries can play havoc with your memory. When you're under pressure, be prepared for memory tasks to be harder as your system floods with stress chemicals and your resources are directed towards basic survival. But also, do everything you can to stay calm and let your brain be brilliant. Adrenaline will energize you, but you also need to replenish your mental reserves if you're going to use your brain at its best. Use your trained imagination to help you relax, beat distractions of every kind, and concentrate on the tough tasks at hand.

3 Find a place of calm

Your learning environment is always important, but it takes on special significance in difficult times. When you're rushed and tired, it's all too easy to neglect physical comfort, but that can be a big mistake, making it even harder to use your memory well. You should be putting more effort than ever into giving yourself a working zone that boosts your thinking: organized and calm, supporting left-brained, logical thought, but also energizing and inspiring so that your right-brain skills are being used at their best. The more chaotic life becomes, the more crucial it is to have a place where you can think, learn and remember.

4 Keep your brain in balance

During your training, you've learnt the importance of 'global thinking': using both 'sides' of your brain to drive your memory. When the pressure's on, at home or in business, there's a danger that one side or the other takes over. Either you put too much effort into left-brained thinking, trying to structure ordered solutions and relying on logical memory techniques, or you retreat too far into your imagination and become unfocused and vague. To survive and thrive, you need to keep the two sides balanced, bringing them together to operate all the memory methods you've developed this week.

5 Write lists and store them as stories

In testing times, there's more to remember, and more to be gained by feeling organized and on track. The 'memory story' technique you've been practising is great for remembering lists of jobs to do, people to call, things to talk about, facts to have at your fingertips. Turn all the important information into memorable images, then link those images into the sort of story you'll recall whenever you need it. Used well, your memory will help you feel organized, save you time, and let you achieve more. You'll impress everyone you meet with your ability to learn new facts, concepts and skills.

6 Work the numbers

Tough economic times make it essential to have a good head for figures. Whether you're negotiating new deals, finding bargains, presenting updated business plans, or just coping with extra phone numbers, serial codes, meeting times and dates, you can reap huge rewards from having even a simple system for remembering numbers. Keep practising the techniques you've explored this week, finding your favourite ways to turn numbers into pictures and then fixing them firmly in your mind. Use your memory to hold onto key numbers, but also to explore and juggle them so that you make good decisions, establish solid contacts and secure winning deals.

7 Map out your mind

When you're pushing yourself to achieve more than ever before, use the ancient 'memory journeys' system to bring extra structure and solidity to your thinking. Design routes based on buildings, walks, streets and cities you know well, and fill them with images to jog your memory about anything and everything you need to know – in exactly the right order to be used to maximum effect. Memory journeys have helped learners for centuries. Whether you're taking exams as you retrain, practising complex new systems and skills, or just managing larger amounts of information, memory journeys can give you all the confidence, speed and flexibility of recall you need today.

8 Be a people person

Life may be tough – but you're not in it alone. There are many people you already know who can help you succeed, if you remember to ask them, and know how to make contact. And there are many more to meet in the near future – so you'll want to remember as much about them as you can. Make sure you hear their name; then be interested in them, find out memorable information, start thinking in pictures, and create links between the person in front of you and the weird and wonderful memory tricks you invent.

9 Talk the talk

In uncertain times, it's great to feel sure about your communication skills. The brain-training you've done this week will help you to make a memorable impression on the people you meet; and when competition is high, the way you present yourself can make a huge difference in meetings, presentations, interviews – even phone-calls. Plan exactly what you want to say, then turn your notes into trigger images to slot into familiar mental routes, helping you to say everything you want to in an organized and powerful way. Memory techniques keep the key facts and figures at your fingertips, let you talk to time and answer questions with confidence, and ensure that you're the person people listen to, trust – and remember.

10 Keep learning

These days we all need to face new challenges and adapt to change. Sometimes that change is unexpected. Maybe you need to master new systems or thrive in a very different working environment. But sometimes it's up to you to make the first move: to *choose* to learn the extra language, take the next professional qualification, master the software and train the rest of the team... do whatever it takes to stay one step ahead. Your new memory skills will help you to survive these testing times, but you'll need to keep the training going – so keep looking for ways to learn more, and learn better. Commit to using your memory well in the long term – and enjoying the process – and you'll put yourself in the very best position to cope with whatever lies ahead.

Notes

ALSO AVAILABLE IN THE 'IN A WEEK' SERIES

BODY LANGUAGE FOR MANAGEMENT • BOOKKEEPING AND ACCOUNTING • CUSTOMER CARE • SPEED READING • DEALING WITH DIFFICULT PEOPLE • EMOTIONAL INTELLIGENCE • FINANCE FOR NON-FINANCIAL MANAGERS • INTRODUCING MANAGEMENT • MANAGING YOUR BOSS • MARKET RESEARCH • NEURO-LINGUISTIC PROGRAMMING • OUTSTANDING CREATIVITY • PLANNING YOUR CAREER • SUCCEEDING AT INTERVIEWS • SUCCESSFUL APPRAISALS • SUCCESSFUL ASSERTIVENESS • SUCCESSFUL BUSINESS PLANS • SUCCESSFUL CHANGE MANAGEMENT • SUCCESSFUL COACHING • SUCCESSFUL COPYWRITING • SUCCESSFUL CVS • SUCCESSFUL INTERVIEWING

For information about other titles in the series, please visit www.inaweek.co.uk

ALSO AVAILABLE IN THE 'IN A WEEK' SERIES

SUCCESSFUL JOB APPLICATIONS • SUCCESSFUL JOB HUNTING
• SUCCESSFUL KEY ACCOUNT MANAGEMENT • SUCCESSFUL LEADERSHIP
• SUCCESSFUL MARKETING • SUCCESSFUL MARKETING PLANS
• SUCCESSFUL MEETINGS • SUCCESSFUL MEMORY TECHNIQUES
• SUCCESSFUL MENTORING • SUCCESSFUL NEGOTIATING • SUCCESSFUL
NETWORKING • SUCCESSFUL PEOPLE SKILLS • SUCCESSFUL
PRESENTING • SUCCESSFUL PROJECT MANAGEMENT • SUCCESSFUL
PSYCHOMETRIC TESTING • SUCCESSFUL PUBLIC RELATIONS •
SUCCESSFUL RECRUITMENT • SUCCESSFUL SELLING • SUCCESSFUL
STRATEGY • SUCCESSFUL TIME MANAGEMENT • TACKLING INTERVIEW
QUESTIONS

For information about other titles in the series, please visit www.inaweek.co.uk

**LEARN IN A WEEK,
WHAT THE EXPERTS
LEARN IN A LIFETIME**

For information about other titles
in the series, please visit
www.inaweek.co.uk